FROM A
MUSTARD
SEED

FROM A
MUSTARD
SEED

ENLIVENING WORSHIP AND MUSIC
IN THE SMALL CHURCH

BRUCE G. EPPERLY
AND
DARYL HOLLINGER

THE
ALBAN
INSTITUTE
HERNDON, VIRGINIA
WWW.ALBAN.ORG

The Alban Institute
2121 Cooperative Way, Suite 100
Herndon, VA 20171

Unless otherwise noted, all Scripture quotations are from the New Revised Standard Version of the Bible, copyright © 1989, Division of Christian Education of the National Council of the Churches of Christ in the United States of America, and are used by permission.

Library of Congress Cataloging-in-Publication Data

Epperly, Bruce Gordon.
  From a mustard seed : enlivening worship and music in the small church / by Bruce Epperly and Daryl Hollinger.
      p. cm.
  Includes bibliographical references (p. 205) and index.
  ISBN 978-1-56699-406-4 (alk. paper)
  1. Small churches. 2. Public worship. 3. Church music. I. Hollinger, Daryl. II. Title.
  BV637.8.E67 2010
  264--dc22
                                    2010021089

    10   11   12   13   14   VP   5   4   3   2   1

CONTENTS

FOREWORD

"WHERE TWO OR THREE are gathered together in my name, there I am in the midst of them." Usually a church member or pastor quotes Matthew 18:20 only when a handful of people show up for a business meeting or a choir rehearsal. Citing this scripture on such occasions is a way of making the most of a disappointing situation when you had hoped for many more participants and greater participation. In the context of Matthew 18, however, this was a statement of encouragement and empowerment rather than the acknowledgement of a disheartening situation. Earlier in the chapter Jesus had turned the power structures on end by stating that those who are child-like will hold the greatest position in the kingdom of heaven (verses 1-6). Then, just as intriguing, Jesus promises to fulfill the prayers of two who pray together and come to an agreement (verse 19). This is the power of consensus in the Spirit.

Like one with the faith of a mustard seed that could move mountains (Matthew 17:20), we are reminded that the kingdom of God is not dependant upon vast numbers. Good things or, as the authors say, beautiful things happen among those who are faithful to God and love each other as brothers and sisters in Christ. The vision of the kingdom of God proposed in

Matthew 18—becoming childlike and reaching consensus in Christ's name—may be even more likely in smaller than larger congregations.

Bruce Epperly and Daryl Hollinger offer us a vision for faithful and fruitful worship and music in smaller congregations that rings with authenticity and delight—authenticity because this vision comes from two people engaged effectively in ministry with smaller congregations, and delight not only because they have accepted the possibilities that smaller congregations might offer, but also have embraced the possibilities of becoming the body of Christ gathered for worship, though in smaller numbers than often thought significant.

I recently had a conversation with a friend and clergywoman who lamented her departure from a rural, blue-collar congregation of 50 members. She felt that her ministry with these people was the most fulfilling and creative of any time in her life. She had entered a period of discernment and though she was sure that the Spirit was calling upon her to refocus her ministry in other areas, leaving this particular body of Christ, though smaller, rural, and less affluent than others, was a struggle.

This book reminds us that a particular body of Christ is not like a Starbucks franchise that may be closed not because it is not profitable, but because it isn't profitable enough. God's yardstick has nothing to do with numbers, but with two short but significant assumptions: Love God with all your heart and love your neighbor as yourself (Matthew 22:37-39).

Indeed vital and faithful congregations may be larger. Size is not an indicator of significance in God's realm. The spectacular aspects of worship characteristic of some larger congregations are not a gauge of spiritual vitality. The authors remind us of the special gifts that are perhaps available much more readily to smaller congregations.

Here we have a rare combination of two authors with complementary ministries and perspectives. First, they offer us a witness of what they are doing: they are engaged and invite us to join them. They offer us their experience and expertise: they are knowledgeable and share generously from their experience. Most of all, they are visionary: they offer us a glimpse of what might be and empower us to claim that vision.

Their vision is one of partnership. Few, if any, staff members receive fulltime salaries in smaller congregations. Bi-vocational ministry is a much more prevalent calling than is generally recognized. This book admirably points out that bi-vocational leadership does not mean that planning need be haphazard and that worship less effective. It does mean that partnership between the pastor and those who lead music is essential for effective ministry. The exploration of the gifts of as many persons as possible is a sine qua non for sustained leadership that avoids burnout.

One of the unique features of this book is that Daryl Hollinger offers a vision for music ministry that contains depth and breadth and, in doing so, honors music's role in shaping a healthy congregational piety and vibrant worship identity. Daryl proposes a diet that reaches deep into the historical tradition of the church and extends broadly to a wide variety of current cultures, both within the United States and beyond. This approach is especially important for smaller congregations who either may feel isolated from the broader church or choose regretfully to exist as a remnant, exiled from the fullness of their heritage and the richness of the universal church.

Bruce Epperly in turn empowers church musicians and congregational members as theologians—partners in the process of developing a theologically articulate congregation. Church musicians play a crucial role in the educational process of a congregation and need to claim this power in making musical decisions.

As the authors indicate, this is hard work. But as Matthew 17 and 18 reminds us, we have considerable power at our disposal. The benchmark of God's realm is not one of size, but faithfulness to God and love for one's neighbor. We are only asked to sow the seeds of love for God and each other. The Spirit joins us in this task and empowers us for this journey.

C. Michael Hawn
University Distinguished Professor of Church Music
Perkins School of Theology
Southern Methodist University
Dallas, Texas

PREFACE

WE BELIEVE THAT small churches can do great things in worship and music. Like the mustard seed of Jesus's parable, small congregations often underestimate their own talents until they discover that God is at work in them, inviting them to share God's good news in worship, word, and act. In the chapters ahead, we will share our experiences working with small congregations that are discovering their many gifts for worship and service. They have found that small can be beautiful in worship as well as congregational life.

This book emerged initially from our work with the Enlivening Worship and Music Program of Lancaster Theological Seminary. We are grateful to the pastors and congregational leaders who participated in this program for their willingness to explore new ways of worship and to share with us their joys and struggles to be faithful Christians. We are especially grateful to the Calvin Institute of Christian Worship, whose generous grant enabled us to initiate our program. We are most especially grateful for the guidance and support of John Witvliet and Betty Grit of the Calvin Institute of Christian Worship.

Lancaster Theological Seminary is a small seminary with the great mission of theological education for every generation.

President Riess Potterveld and Dean Edwin David Aponte provided invaluable support and encouragement throughout this project. Bruce's colleagues in the Office of Continuing Education provided worship, logistical, and marketing assistance. We are especially grateful to Rev. Kathy Harvey Nelson, April Bupp, and Brenda Marin for their support.

We are thankful to Richard Bass and Beth Gaede at the Alban Institute and to our copy editor Jean Caffey Lyles for their commitment to supporting us in our quest for excellence in the writing of this text.

Both of us are grateful for the creativity and commitment of our respective Lancaster, Pennsylvania, congregations, St. Peter's United Church of Christ and Disciples United Community Church.

This work would not have been possible apart from the loving support of our wives and partners in ministry. Rev. Bonnie Hollinger led worship during many of our Enlivening Worship and Music seminars and provided energy and inspiration throughout this project. Rev. Kate Epperly's support and pastoral wisdom were helpful beyond words.

We dedicate this book to our respective fathers, Everett L. Epperly and Elam B. Hollinger, both pastors who faithfully led small congregations and sought to be true to their callings; and also to the many pastors, worship leaders, and congregations that are seeking to give glory to God through faithful worship and service.

CHAPTER 1

THE SMALL CHURCH

BEAUTIFUL AND CHALLENGING

We believe that small congregations can be God's partners in creating vital and life-transforming worship and music. The two of us are committed to supporting small congregations in their quest to embrace and embody lively new ways of worshiping, because we believe that God is present in every congregation and every person, actively seeking healing, wholeness, and abundant life. Despite the challenges that small congregations, averaging less than seventy-five in worship, face—including limited resources and participation—small-membership congregations can experience God's new creation when they discover their unique gifts and explore innovative ways to share in God's vision through mission and worship. Small is challenging—but it can also be beautiful!

Each Saturday evening, Bruce's congregation, Disciples United Community Church (DUCC), an emerging congregation[1] in Lancaster, Pennsylvania, affiliated with the United Church of Christ and the Christian Church (Disciples of Christ), concludes its worship service with the celebration of communion. At DUCC, Word and Sacrament are seamlessly joined as the sermon theme flows into the offering and pastoral prayers, and then into the celebration of communion as God's invitation to all people who seek to follow Jesus. Each

1

Saturday's communion is a festive celebration of the resurrection for this faithful community of thirty to forty worshipers gathered around the brightly adorned communion table. But on one particular Saturday, the experience of Christ's resurrection came to our congregation in an unexpected way. In the spirit of the congregation's open communion, in which those of all ages and backgrounds are invited to experience Christ's presence in sharing the bread and the cup, a toddler was given a large piece of communion bread. Before he had a chance to bite into it, his father dipped the bread into the chalice containing grape juice. For a moment, the two-year-old stared at the purple bread, perplexed by this colorful new ingredient. Then, as he took a bite of the bread of life and savored the flavor of the cup of salvation, his face was transformed from puzzlement to joy. The whole community broke into spontaneous laughter as we witnessed the unexpected and contagious joy of Christ's resurrection revealed in the everyday elements of bread and juice. A little child had led us into experiencing the meaning of the psalmist's affirmation, "taste and see that [God] is good" (Ps. 34:8). Though we were few—just a couple of dozen that evening—we knew that the God of beauty, power, and glory was in our midst. In that moment, our worship embraced the fullness of God's new creation of heaven and earth. We experienced ourselves as being part of God's abundant life through which small congregations can do great things.

FAITHFUL WORSHIP
IN SMALL CONGREGATIONS

Such life-transforming moments happen regularly in small congregations. At a gathering of pastors and worship leaders involved in the Enlivening Worship and Music in the Small Church program, sponsored by Lancaster Theological Seminary and the Calvin Institute of Christian Worship, one participant told of a joyful moment in her congregation of fifty worshipers. After the six-member choir sang the anthem one Sunday morning, a two-year-old clapped and burst out, "Hooray!" Her delighted affirmation reminded the fifty congregants that, despite the small size of their congregation, they had gathered that morning for only one reason—to praise God and joyfully acknowledge God's beauty, love, and grace as a community of friends and neighbors. What the adults in the congregation had judged as a small and struggling choir, this child experienced as the voice of the angels! God was truly in this place of worship and, despite all the challenges this congregation faced, now the people knew it. In that moment of call and response, this congregation was experiencing the meaning of the psalmist's affirmation, "Let everything that breathes praise God" (Ps. 150:6).

Yes, worship in small churches can be challenging, but it can also be beautiful. In the course of this book, the two of us will share a vision of faithful and vital congregations, all of which would be described as small in membership. Some are declining numerically as a result of changing small-town or inner-city demographics; others are just barely holding their own but wondering what the next decade will bring; still others have been small but stable throughout their history. Some small congregations are found in rural communities, others in county-seat towns, and still others in suburbs or in the inner city.

As the two of us work with pastors and laypeople involved in Lancaster Theological Seminary's various congregational adult-education, worship, and ministerial excellence and transformation programs, we have discovered that small congregations can plan meaningful worship and music that give comfort, provide guidance, and inspire transformation through all the seasons of life.[2] We have also discovered that pastors and worship leaders can guide their congregations to new ways of worship that mirror their congregation's theology and call congregants to new ways of experiencing God's presence in their lives. While it is easy to overlook the gifts of small congregations, the biblical tradition reminds us that from a mere mustard seed, a great tree can grow, and from a modest lunch pail of five loaves and two fish, a multitude can be fed.

Although small congregations are often limited by feelings of scarcity and memories of past glories, we believe that small congregations can share in God's abundant life through faithful, theologically grounded, and innovative worship services. As pastors of small Canadian congregations, Peter Bush and Christine O'Reilly note, "Worship is the nourishing center of the congregation's life," whether twenty-five or two thousand are gathered for worship.[3] Each week, small congregations come together to sing their faith, share God's good news, and join hands in prayers of praise, gratitude, and intercession. As they face the challenges of small membership, limited resources, and budget constraints, small churches everywhere still give voice each week to God's faithfulness in every season of life.

OBSTACLES TO VITAL WORSHIP IN SMALL CONGREGATIONS

While great things happen each week in small churches, such congregations also face great difficulties in fulfilling their mission. Just listen to the testimonies of these faithful pastors and laypeople. A Western Pennsylvania pastor noted:

> Many members of my congregation are still grieving the loss of young adults and children in worship. They know that young families are leaving our town to find educational opportunities and better jobs elsewhere. But they still reminisce about the good old days when there were twenty members in the choir and thirty children raced up to hear the children's sermon. Now the five-member choir sings only at special services, and we're lucky to have two children come forward for the children's sermon. How can I help them see that wherever two or three or fifty are gathered for worship, God can do great things?

An active lay member from Maryland observes that her congregation resists any change the pastor wants to make, whether in hymns or the order of worship.

> I don't know if they're afraid of change or just holding onto something familiar in a rapidly changing world. I've heard some members suggest that if we just return to the old ways of doing things in worship, this will bring back children and young parents. But I don't think so! Unless we move ahead, we'll slide backward.

A United Church of Christ pastor from the Pocono Mountains of Northeastern Pennsylvania notes:

> People in our church wonder why we haven't grown like the Worship Center outside of town. "What's wrong with us?" they ask. "Is it the worship service, our message, or the pastor's sermons?" I know that they don't want to be like the Worship Center, theologically or in worship style, but they want to grow just enough to stay even, and are worried that all the young people will want to go where there's a praise band, PowerPoint, and movie clips each Sunday.

A United Methodist pastor from Central Maryland reflects:

> The problem at our church is passivity. Folks want to observe rather than participate in worship. Apart from our choir, no one volunteers to read Scripture or help with the children's sermon. I don't want to be the center of the service, winding them up each Sunday morning. It's not just about me and my leadership; it's about the people of our church living in relationship with God and each other in praise and worship.

Do any of these comments describe the worship life of your congregation? Although the majority of Protestant congregations in the United States and Canada have fewer than seventy-five participants in worship each week, small churches struggle to affirm God's abundant life in their attitudes toward worship, adult education, and financial and human resources. Small churches often think small, while God calls them to think big as they consider their worship, mission, and fellowship. They forget that God's call to faithfulness embraces small congregations as well as megachurches.

Bush and O'Reilly note the many challenges small congregations face in their book *Where Twenty or Thirty Are Gathered: Leading Worship in the Small Church*:

- Perceived self-limitation
- Burnout among leaders
- Focus on survival rather than mission
- History that limits rather than inspires
- Lack of resources in finances and people
- Fear of trying new things
- Unrealistic expectations about future growth
- Inability to respond creatively to changes in the community[4]

Take a moment to consider your own congregation's attitudes toward worship and mission. Do these challenges sound familiar? Does your church face any—or all—of the spiritual, personnel, or attitudinal challenges described by Bush and O'Reilly? Small congregations, like individuals, can define themselves by perceived limitations even though God promises them abundant life. They can hold onto bygone days when God is calling them toward a hopeful future. As a frustrated layperson noted:

> We're living in the past at this church. Just the thought of a new hymnal to supplement the hymnal we've had for nearly fifty years brings out all the naysayers in the congregation. I hear them say, "It's too hard to learn new hymns," "We like

things just the way they are," or "Why do we have to change? Can't the young people be satisfied with our music?"

Another layperson, active in a declining urban congregation in a major East Coast city, notes the double bind that often paralyzes small congregations:

> We want to grow, but we don't want to change. We're depressed by what we've become, but we don't want to try anything that might help us reach out to the neighborhood as well as grow spiritually in new ways.

A third layperson noted the ambivalence experienced in many small congregations:

> When many of our members look at the current participants, all they see is gray hair and only a few young couples. They don't see the treasures hidden in the forty people gathered here each week. We're small, but we have some good readers, singers, and maybe even a few talented musicians. If we take a chance, we can do something beautiful here! We don't have to be perfect to be good enough!

Once upon a time, Jesus asked a man who had been lying beside a healing pool for nearly forty years, waiting for the right moment to be healed, "Do you want to be made well?" (John 5:6). The man responded with good reasons why he was still paralyzed. We suspect that Jesus sympathized with his problems and accepted his reasons as legitimate, but Jesus also challenged him with a new vision of reality, commanding him, "Stand up, take your mat, and walk" (John 5:8). Today God may be asking your congregation the same question. "Do you want to have vital worship? Do you want to be more attuned to God's presence in your congregation's worship and spiritual life? Do you want to praise God in new and life-giving ways?" While your congregation may give all sorts of legitimate reasons for the realities of shrinking membership or lifeless worship, we believe that God may be calling your congregation to go forward toward God's future, to risk exploring new forms of worship, and to trust that God has given you all the spiritual gifts you need to be faithful and imaginative in worship, prayer, and music.

The two of us believe that God is always challenging people and congregations to move faithfully toward the future that God is imagining for us. When congregations and their leaders trust in God's abundant life, they will discover the truth of Paul's promise to the small congregation at Philippi, "God will fully satisfy every need of yours according to [God's] riches in glory in Christ Jesus" (Phil. 4:19). Even if your congregation is small and unlikely to grow significantly in membership, God is present in your church, providing all the resources and inspiration you need to be faithful and creative in worship. Through the words of the apostle Paul, God still challenges congregations of all sizes with the affirmation, "Do not be conformed to this world, but be transformed by the renewing of your minds" (Rom. 12:2).

Take another moment to look long and hard at your congregation's life. To which outworn traditions is your congregation "conformed"? What limits has the congregation placed upon itself? Are these limits realistic, or are there new possibilities for growth and adventure hidden within these limits? When you look at your congregation, what would be the first step—even a small one—it could take in transforming worship and music?

As you ponder these questions, remember that God's call to your congregation is to be faithful to its unique vocation, given its particular community and tradition. As small congregations ponder how they can be faithful to God's calling in their life together, they need to recall the words of a Jewish proverb, attributed to the Hasidic sage Rabbi Zusya, who once said that "in the next world, the Messiah will not ask 'why were you not Moses?' but 'why were you not Zusya?'" That's God's question to every small congregation: Will you live out your unique calling, rather than comparing yourself with larger and more financially prosperous congregations? Will you be faithful to my gifts right where you are and in the people you see each Sunday morning? After all, you don't need to be a megachurch to have megatheology and megaworship!

VITAL WORSHIP IN SMALL CONGREGATIONS

Worship and music in small congregations can be innovative, lively, and beautiful. While small churches often suffer from a failure of imagination, their size may enable them to become agents of transformation, beginning with small steps that often lead to great changes in worship, music, preaching, and community life. As Bush and O'Reilly note, small congregations, despite all their limitations, can be "intimate, flexible, and participatory."[5] Within these unique characteristics, the seeds of growth lie hidden, just waiting to germinate and burst forth in fruitful, faithful, and life-giving worship, whether in times of celebration or occasions of sorrow.

Following our first seminar on enlivening worship and music in the small church, one of the pastors reported that in just a few weeks' time, "our choir quit wearing its 1950s choir robes and transformed itself into a praise and worship group." Another congregation decided to change its approach to planning Advent worship. While preserving the congregation's healthy traditions, its worship team chose to include dramatic presentations and global music in its preparation for Christ's coming into the world.[6] A third congregation, whose sanctuary seated two hundred, chose to rope off the last five rows so that the fifty congregants could sing together as a choir. While a few members grumbled at the new seating arrangements, the results of changing the worship space were gratifying. Members began to appreciate each others' voices and, to their amazement, the quality of music in worship was transformed. These are small changes in the scheme of things, but as every traveler knows, small steps can lead to adventurous journeys.

Both of us are children of small congregations. Bruce grew up in the 1950s in the Community Baptist Church in King City, California. In this small American Baptist congregation where his father, Everett Epperly, served as pastor, Bruce always looked forward to communion on the first Sunday of the month. Following the sermon, each congregant was served a small cracker and a cup of grape juice. Nearly fifty years have passed since Bruce's childhood in California's Salinas Valley, but he still remembers his father saying at the conclusion of communion, "And when they sang a hymn, they went out," as a prelude to singing the Baptist standard "Blest Be the Tie that Binds." He remembers the faith given voice by that small congregation of farmers, ranchers, and small-business owners. Looking back nearly five decades, Bruce can still visualize the faces of that gathered community and the importance the simple worship service played in helping people face disappointment, illness, and death with a sense of God's faithful and sustaining presence. Each Sunday, they were called to trust God's guiding presence and to live by the words of faith they regularly sang in worship, whether facing death, burying a loved one, dealing with drought, or struggling with chronic illness.

Several years later, as a college student, Bruce attended Grace Baptist Church in San Jose, California. This small, progressive congregation lived out the spirit of "Blest Be the Tie that Binds" as it responded faithfully to joys and sorrows within the congregation and the world. This congregation of seventy provided Bruce with a spiritual home, gave him leadership roles, and set him on the first steps of a path that led to ordained ministry and seminary leadership. As a college sophomore, Bruce preached his first sermon at Grace Baptist on Laity Sunday. While he is glad that no tapes or transcripts of this sermon remain in existence, he is grateful for a small congregation that saw his gifts, gave him the chance to develop them, and blessed him with no-interest loans that enabled him to attend seminary and graduate school without incurring significant debt.

As he remembers worship at Grace Baptist Church, Bruce recalls the smiles that broke out on people's faces whenever a member testified to a job offer or a recovery from illness. He also remembers the audible sighs of pain and empathy that went through the congregation when it was reported that an elderly member had been hospitalized or a young mother had been diagnosed with cancer. He still recalls how this small congregation made a difference in the larger community through its integration of faith and action, whether in initiating an urban ministry in response to the changing neighborhood, speaking out against the Vietnam War and providing counseling for conscientious objectors, welcoming the growing number of people released into the community from mental-health institutions, or supporting the struggle for justice among California farmworkers.

In this small manifestation of the body of Christ, each Sunday's worship brought together seventy-five people who lived out the meaning of Paul's affirmation, "If one member suffers, all suffer together with it; if one member is honored, all rejoice together with it" (1 Cor. 12:26). In great appreciation for the worship of these small churches, Bruce affirms:

> I learned the meaning of faithful ministry at Grace Baptist Church from faithful pastors like John Akers and George L. Collins, who sought to live out the gospel in the context of the social changes of the sixties and early seventies and from laypeople like Geneva Vaughan, Henry Jensen, and Claude Keith who embraced, not without struggle, innovative worship and reached out to the changing neighborhood. The church always struggled to make budget; but it always lived the spirit of its name, "Grace," as it reached out rather than turned inward, even in the most difficult financial times. Although there was a time when Grace Baptist boasted two

services and four hundred congregants at Sunday services, I never heard anyone reminisce about the good old days. Faithfulness to their progressive vision gave the members courage to take risks and do new things in worship and in the community. Small can be beautiful when you live by grace.

True to its mission to share God's grace with a changing community, Grace Baptist was open to change with the times, whether in the arrangement of pews, the style of worship, or the welcoming of gay and lesbian couples. God was alive in handshakes and hymn sings, in service and sharing, in preaching and prayer. Grace Baptist's leaders were inspired by one affirmation that kept them going in times of plenty and scarcity: "God is working in our church toward a future greater than we can imagine." Though at opposite ends of the theological spectrum, both Baptist congregations embodied the spirit of the communion hymn Bruce learned in childhood:

> Blest be the tie that binds
> our hearts in Christian love;
> the fellowship of kindred minds
> is like to that above.[7]

Also a child of the fifties and sixties, Daryl was shaped by a small congregation in the early years of his childhood. His father was a church planter in rural communities of southern Alabama. One of his churches, Grace Fellowship, was a small body of new converts. Daryl has vivid memories of worship services in the cinder-block meetinghouse—his mother at the piano and his father in the pulpit. Many services were evangelistic. Songs like "Jesus Saves," "Leaning on the Everlasting Arms," and "Amazing Grace" were staples of worship. The singing was heartfelt and spirited. The singers' voices swooned and slid in an emotional fervor that reflected the culture of the Deep South.

The baptism services, a vivid memory for Daryl, were held by the banks of Burnt Corn Creek, where fifteen to twenty new converts were baptized. The converts were taken about waist-deep into the creek, where Daryl's father and the Sunday school superintendent immersed each of them in the cool water. As a young child, Daryl perceived those services as happy, playful moments. While the small assembly sang songs like "Shall We Gather at the River," Daryl played along the creek's edge. He remembers the smell of creosote from the wooden planks of the old bridge. The water was refreshing and crystal clear as the smooth pebbles in the creek glistened in the sunlight. It was a delightful time for Daryl; from those services he first learned about spontaneity, joy, and playfulness in worship.

When Daryl was seven, his family returned to Pennsylvania, where his father became associate pastor of a small Mennonite church. Years later, as a new high-school graduate, Daryl went with his father back to Grace Fellowship to hold evangelistic services. This time, Daryl was the song and worship leader. The small size and welcoming spirit of Grace Fellowship provided a safe environment for Daryl to build confidence in his own talents as a musician. Today, as Daryl creates imaginative worship in his own small congregation, St. Peter's United Church of Christ in Lancaster, Pennsylvania, he is reminded of the way his gifts were used as a youth. The music and the sharing of simple gifts reflected the congregation's culture; they enabled Daryl's leadership to be embraced and supported. This was the beginning of his long and creative ministry as a church musician.

In Daryl's workshops on enlivening worship in the small church, the influence of Grace Fellowship is often felt. While leading songs like "Shall We Gather at the River," Daryl remembers the gospel flavor of that little rural church. He urges singers not to worry about hitting the notes squarely, but to sing with spirit and to let the music move with the natural inflections of the human voice. He encourages the musicians to slow the tempo, so the piano can be played in a gospel-style waltz; he elicits spontaneity through improvisation and playfulness in the music. Singing in the spirit of rural America can bring another lens to the old gospel songs. It allows congregations to experience worship from a different time and place. Our singing may take on a new emotional fervor and personal devotion when we capture the spirit of revival singing.

Now, decades later, Daryl's ministry is still shaped by that tiny body of believers at Grace Fellowship. He is grateful for those simple beginnings where he experienced God's love in community and saw firsthand how a small church expressed its faith in heartfelt worship and song. These memories spur him on today in his mission to invite congregations to live out their theology and piety with honesty, vitality, and integrity.

Following the example of the small churches in which he grew up, Daryl is committed to enriching worship in small congregations by nurturing gifts that are already present among the members. He believes that even though choirs may be small and resources limited, music and worship may still be beautiful and inspiring.

O'Reilly and Bush note that small churches faithfully embody the good news of personal transformation and community outreach. "Small churches have long practiced a spirituality that was applied, relational, and life-changing."[8] When small congregations are tempted to dwell on their obvious limitations in size and resources, we are quick to respond that great possibilities lie hidden within every mustard seed as we remind them of the gifts of small congregations:

- ✦ Intimacy born of face-to-face encounters over a lifetime
- ✦ Rapid communication among members
- ✦ A shared history of joys and sorrows
- ✦ Hospitality both within and beyond the congregation
- ✦ Faithful witness in challenging environments
- ✦ The presence of senior adults who have faithfully followed the gospel for decades

- ◆ Family spirit
- ◆ Generosity within and beyond the congregation
- ◆ Opportunities for people of all ages to lead and share gifts in worship and community life[9]

Last but not least, worship is at the heart of congregational life in small churches. Small-church worship is holistic as it joins intimacy, often the fruit of decades of shared ministry, through the sharing of song, thanksgiving, reflection, service, and friendship. In the spirit of the popular television series *Cheers*, small churches are places "where everyone knows your name." While such "family" settings can at times be patriarchal, slow to change, systemically dysfunctional, and oppressive, small family congregations also provide a face-to-face and cradle-to-grave intimacy and compassion that is rare in current North American culture. Still, at their best, small congregations joyfully affirm in song and ritual a faith that transforms lives, gives comfort to those who grieve, and enables people to trust God's care as they face their final moments.

Yes, the two of us recognize that the quest to enliven worship and music in small congregations can be difficult, but we recognize something more profound in the worship of small congregations, and this reality inspires our work with small congregations and their leaders. We recognize that God is still working in our world and in our congregations to bring forth healing, justice, and abundant life, and that small churches have a vocation to fulfill as partners in God's great work of wholeness and adventure. In the pages ahead, we will share our vision of ways that small congregations can do great things in sharing God's grace and salvation through worship and music with their existing resources. The path ahead for many small congregations is a struggle, but they can go forth in faith, knowing that they are companions with God on a surprising, holy adventure of faithful worship and service.

ENLIVENING WORSHIP AND MUSIC IN YOUR CHURCH

We will conclude each chapter with a spiritual practice that integrates theology, worship, and prayer. We believe that enlivening worship and music in small churches involves the dynamic and creative synthesis of prayer, imagination, and practice. When we ground congregational transformation in prayer, we discover that we have the resources to honor tradition and embrace innovation for the glory of God and the growth of our congregations.

Praying for Your Congregation

As you begin the adventure of enlivening worship and music in your church, we invite you, first of all, to commit to deepening your prayer life. While the contemplative practices in the Christian tradition are many, we suggest an integration of silence, spiritual affirmations, and intercessory prayer. We invite congregational worship leaders and choir members to covenant to take five minutes each morning to be still in God's presence (Ps. 46:10), anticipating that God will provide inspiration and guidance. We invite you, after a time of silence, to pray for the lay and pastoral leadership of your congregation, either through visualizing each person or by naming each in God's presence. We then invite you to take a moment to pray for the congregation as a whole with special concern for its worship service. Rather than emphasizing what the congregation lacks in resources and talent, trust in God's abundant life moving within the congregation. Take a few moments to visualize the worship service as a time for lively prayer and praise in which the participants experience God's grace in Scripture, song, and spoken word. Conclude this time of prayer by thanking God for the many gifts and talents within your congregation.

A further way of embodying the prayerful quest for lively and transformative worship in small congregations involves inviting each member of the congregation to pray for its worship service as he or she awakens on Sunday morning and to begin each Sunday morning with a sense of expectation and hope. Remind the congregation that the pastor and worship leaders are empowered and inspired by the prayers of the faithful. When we pray, we open the doors for God to provide new and lively possibilities for congregational transformation. As the United Church of Christ motto notes, "God is still speaking." God is already present in our worship and awaits our awareness and response.

Affirming Your Congregation's Gifts

The apostle Paul counseled a small congregation in Rome: "Do not be conformed to this world, but be transformed by the renewing of your minds, so that you may discern what is the will of God—what is good and acceptable and perfect" (Rom. 12:2). Many small congregations need to move from scarcity to abundance in their self-understanding. Spiritual affirmations can transform both people and communities by awakening them to God's promises for our lives. Small congregations experience new direction and vitality when they follow the apostle Paul's guidance to the small congregation at Philippi:

> Finally, beloved, whatever is true, whatever is honorable, whatever is just, whatever is pure, whatever is pleasing, whatever is commendable, if there is any excellence and if there is anything worthy of praise, think about these things.
> —PHILIPPIANS 4:8

As congregations and worship leaders begin the process of enlivening worship and music, they need to surround themselves with spiritual affirmations.[10] Affirmations are most effective when we say them regularly, especially when we are tempted to live by closed-system scarcity instead of by open-system divine abundance. We suggest the following affirmations as means of transforming and enlivening worship.

> [We] can do all things through [God] who strengthens [us].
> —Philippians 4:13

> My God will satisfy every need of yours according to [God's] riches in glory in Christ Jesus.
> —Philippians 4:19

We trust Jesus's promise:

> I came that they may have life, and have it abundantly.
> —John 10:10

As we commit ourselves to opening to God's presence in our congregation through prayerful and affirmative faith, we will discover new possibilities for vitality, creativity, and growth where we once saw only limitation.

CHAPTER 2

GLORY AND GRATITUDE AND PRAISE

THEOLOGY AND WORSHIP IN THE SMALL CHURCH

PHILOSOPHER ALFRED NORTH Whitehead once stated that "The worship of God is not a rule of safety—it is an adventure of the spirit, a flight after the unattainable. The death of religion comes with the suppression of the high hope of adventure."[1] While small congregations often want to cling to the safety of still waters, the vision of vital and life-transforming worship and music calls them to an "adventure of the spirit," which is at the heart of the gospel message. When they are confronted by God's call to launch out into deeper waters, many small church leaders first respond in ways similar to the disciple Peter: "Master, we have worked all night long but have caught nothing" (Luke 5:5a). But despite their reasons for hanging onto old patterns of worship, Christ gives small congregations a vision of faithful worship and service. New patterns of faithful worship surface as small congregations leave the shallow waters of familiarity to venture forth as partners in God's holy adventure. Despite previous failures, small but adventurous congregations will respond, in the spirit of the apostle Peter, "Yet, if you say so, I will let down the nets" (Luke 5:5b). Trusting God's creative wisdom and loving presence, adventurous congregations will explore new ways of worship and learn unfamiliar hymns and songs. In the process, they will discover an unexpected abundance of congregational vitality and vision that they previously could not have imagined.

Creative, life-affirming, and adventurous worship in small congregations begins with the affirmation that God is present in all things, seeking life-changing relationships with people and communities. For the One who numbers the hairs on our heads and charts the flight of the sparrow, no congregation is too small to be a place of healing, wonder, reconciliation, and mission. The practical meaning of divine omnipresence can be found in the transformational affirmation, "God is present in our church and is giving us the vision and energy to be faithful in worship and service." When small congregations ground their worship planning in the recognition that God is with them, calling them to do great things in worship, "all things are possible" for spiritual and liturgical growth.

At Bruce's congregation, Disciples United Community Church, this sense of active partnership with God in our worship service is reflected in a song that the congregation often repeats during the offering and preparation for communion:

> Now let earth to heaven raise
> Glory and gratitude and praise:
> These we offer to God.[2]

In this chapter, we chart a theology of worship, grounded in practicing glory, gratitude, and praise in personal and congregational life, which together inspire congregational mission to the larger community. The two of us believe that worship is the central act of congregational life and the central vehicle for experiencing and living out the Christian faith in its many dimensions. Regardless of a congregation's theological perspective, we have discovered that practicing faithful and creative worship shapes congregants' theology, lifestyle, and response to unexpected as well as expected challenges of life. Worship turns us toward God's vision for our lives and inspires us toward mission with the world.

WORSHIP AS LIVED THEOLOGY

At Disciples United Community Church, where Bruce serves as co-pastor, new forms of worship that reflect our ecumenical, emerging, and progressive theology have become living examples of the dynamic faith we affirm. The interplay of chants, global music, and meditative prayer, along with theologically grounded preaching and the weekly celebration of communion, have enabled worshipers to grow in their understanding of who God is and what God is calling them to do in our own pluralistic, postmodern age. At St. Peter's United Church of Christ, where Daryl serves as minister of music, lively and easily learned global music has breathed new life into a historic congregation and has inspired the church to see liturgy as the "people's work," not just in worship but also in outreach to the neighborhood, hospitality toward the small ethnic congregations that worship in the building, and sponsorship of several refugee families.

Throughout this book, we will affirm that what we sing, hear, and do in worship truly does matter. While we may not clearly remember many of the details of worship services or sermons over the course of a lifetime, the ongoing interplay of hymns, Scripture, sacrament, and the preached word forms our images of God, attitudes toward suffering, responses to social and political issues, understanding of church-state relationships, and hospitality toward strangers and people of other faith traditions. Worship, like breakfast, is the most important but often least appreciated meal in the diet of Christian community. Day after day, week after week, and year after year, faithful Christians gathering in small congregations find courage to face what they cannot change and hope to inspire them to confront what can be changed in their personal lives and larger communities.

Such courage and hope are nurtured in the interplay of public and communal worship, solitary and contemplative prayer, and spoken word and sung hymns.

Small congregations find energy in healthy face-to-face relationships. Whereas you can be anonymous in midsized and large congregational worship services, in small congregations eventually everyone knows your name and soon finds out the quality of your singing voice or the part you might be asked to sing in a choir of five or seven voices. Incarnational and participatory as they live out the wisdom of 1 Corinthians 12, small churches recognize that everyone present, from the smallest child to the oldest adult, can be a leader. Although they don't often articulate their theological understandings of congregational life, small churches, at their best, experience Christ's presence in everyone, and despite their occasional poor self-images, they are places where it is assumed that both the aged and the young bring their five loaves and two fishes. "All hands on deck" is the motto of small-church worship. When small congregations awaken to the reality of God's presence in worship, they can faithfully affirm, "Everyone brings a gift for worship and service, despite one's age, talent, or health." Each congregant can affirm, "I matter in this church, and so does everyone else!"

HOLISTIC WORSHIP AND THEOLOGY IN THE SMALL CHURCH

The two of us see worship as dynamic and relational. Accordingly, we see the Celtic cross, in which a circle joins the vertical and horizontal dimensions of life, as an inspirational symbol for authentic worship in small congregations. On the one hand, the worship of God turns us toward the "heavens" in search of God's perspective for our lives and the world. As we look toward the heavens, we see signs of God's presence everywhere and in all things. Worship liberates us from self-preoccupation and turns our attention to God's vision for our lives and congregations in such a way that everyone is the focal point of

God's blessing. On the other hand, in worship we discover that right here and now, in this place and time, God loves us and is working in our lives. But—just as important—we discover God's presence and activity in the lives of the neighbor and the stranger, whether she or he is in Tehran, Iran; Beijing, China; Moscow, Russia; Cairo, Egypt; or Mumbai, India.

Whole-person worship reminds us that heaven is not far off but here on earth as we pray and live out the affirmation, "Thy kingdom come, thy will be done, *on earth* as it is in heaven." Contrary to the old adage that assumes faith takes us away from the world, holistic theologies of worship proclaim, "When we *are* heavenly minded, we *are* truly good for the earth!"

Communal worship also orients us toward the world in which we live and the far horizons toward which God calls a pilgrim people. In loving God, we experience holiness in relationship with our neighbors near and far. In inspiring us to love our neighbors, holistic worship reminds us of our vocation as stewards of the earth—stewards whose primary gift to God is the healing quality of our relationships, both in our communities and toward people we will never meet.

An image from sixth-century monastic Dorotheus of Gaza describes the holistic vision of worship in which love of God and creation are united in one lively and all-encompassing movement of grace:

> Suppose we take a compass and insert the point and draw the outline of a circle. The center point is the same distance from any point on the circumference. . . . Let us suppose that this circle is the world and that God is the center: the straight lines drawn from the circumference to the center are the lives of human beings. . . . Let us assume for the sake of analogy that to move toward God, then, human beings move from the circumference along the various radii of the circle to the center. But, at the same time, the closer they are to God, the closer they become to one another; and the closer they are to one another, the closer they become to God.[3]

If God is present everywhere and in all things, then we cannot separate love of God from love of the world, nor can we separate body, mind, and spirit in worship and daily life. Joined in the circle of God's love, symbolized by the circular center of the Celtic cross, the horizontal and vertical beams reflect the focus of our lives in the various components of worship—toward both God and the world as one dynamic and interdependent movement—and not a dualism in which God and the world, or heaven and earth, are separate realities. God is near to us in worship and in everyday life as the loving reality "in [whom] we live and move and have our being" (Acts 17:28) or, as the congregants proclaim at Disciples United Community Church, "God in all things and all things in God."

Christ's incarnation reminds us that everyday life is an ongoing call and response in which God invites us to live faithfully and creatively as God's companions in healing the world. At its best, worship reminds us of God's intimate and ongoing revelation in our lives and inspires us to experience wholeness and wonder in the ordinary and repetitive events of everyday life. To paraphrase spiritual guide Gerald May, in worship we *pause, notice, open, yield, stretch,* and *respond* to the grace that surrounds, accepts, and guides us.[4]

GOD OF GRACE AND GOD OF GLORY

The two of us affirm that holistic congregational worship is profoundly theocentric in nature. In turning toward God in worship, we discover ourselves as we are intended to be, God's beloved children in whom God is well pleased and to whom God provides a vision and vocation for ourselves and the larger world. Participants in small congregations find greater perspective and vocation in the words of Psalm 8:

When I look at the heavens, the work of your fingers,
the moon and the stars that you have established;
what are human beings that you are mindful of them,

mortals that you care for them?
Yet you have made them a little lower than God,
and crowned them with glory and honor.

—Psalm 8:3–5

Awe at the vastness of the universe ironically inspires us to claim God's calling for our lives and congregations right where we are. This contrast of God's grandeur and human finitude characterized Isaiah's encounter with the Living God as he sought guidance in the Jerusalem Temple. While the Scripture does not give the details of Isaiah's experience, it is entirely possible that his mystical experience occurred in the context of temple worship. With worshipers all around him, Isaiah experiences the wonder of the universe: "the whole earth is full of [God's] glory" (Isa. 6:3). But rather than turning inward in ecstasy, Isaiah commits himself to God's mission. When he hears the voice of the Majestic One, "Whom shall I send, and who will go for us?" Isaiah's response is straightforward: "Here am I; send me!" (Isa. 6:8). In the vastness of the universe and the immense cosmic adventure, we as individuals and as congregations have a vocation to share in God's mission.

Worship invites us to experience the wonder of the Creator of all things. We are drawn into God's glory as we proclaim, "Then sings my soul, my Savior, God, to thee, how great thou art," but the God of glory, more majestic than the galaxies, points us earthward in appreciation and mission, inspiring us to chant, "This is my Father's [or Parent's] world." All things are in God, and God is beyond all things. Yet for those who have eyes to see, God is also within all things, and divine omnipresence calls us to serve God in the "least of these," whether across the aisle in church or in the soup kitchen or in a far-off land.

A pastor of a small congregation in Pennsylvania decided to break free of her congregation's word-oriented tradition of worship by bringing in slides of photographs taken from the Hubble telescope. As the congregation sang "How Great Thou Art," she flashed images of galactic beauty upon the screen.

Later, during the time of intercession and thanksgiving, she illuminated pictures of the earth and its inhabitants, including the Grand Canyon, a rainbow, a bird in flight, a newborn child, and the human immune system. In conclusion, she juxtaposed photos of the aftermath of Hurricane Katrina and the faces of people from diverse ethnic groups and nations with pictures of the galaxies. In response to her "radical" transformation of Sunday worship, one longtime member of the congregation exclaimed, "God was real for me today in worship. Somehow, I feel connected to the universe and to people in need, but even more thankful that God cares for me and wants me to help out when I see tragedies." A few small changes in worship inspired a congregational patriarch to consider new faith practices "for the living of these days."

Timaeus of Locris, once asserted, "God is a circle whose center is everywhere and whose circumference is nowhere." Encircled and centered in God's loving embrace, all things reflect God's glory. Faithful worship calls us to awaken to the mysticism of everyday life and then to reach out in mission to bring wholeness to the earth and its inhabitants. Recognition of God's glory and the wonder of life calls congregations to look beyond the boundaries of congregational worship and, thus, inspires among congregants prayerful attentiveness and action to achieve, like Esther, their calling for "just such a time as this" in their communities and the nation. Inspired to faithful praise as they sing words of praise such as "This is my Father's world, and to my listening ears, all nature sings, and round me rings the music of the spheres," congregants in churches of all sizes are challenged to love all those whom God loves and to join in God's healing of all creation.

> Our God has made this world; oh, let us ne'er forget
> that though the wrong seems oft so strong, God is the ruler yet.
> God trusts us with this world, to keep it clean and fair.
> All earth and trees, the sky and seas, God's creatures
>   everywhere.[5]

The glory of "God who stretched the spangled heavens, infinite in time and space,"[6] inspires us in worship to become God's own companions in healthy stewardship of finite, mortal, and fragile creation.

NOW THANK WE ALL OUR GOD

German mystic Meister Eckhardt is reputed to have said, "If the only prayer you make is 'thank you,' that will be sufficient." Without the spirit of thanksgiving, worship degenerates into an individualistic hymn to our own good fortune, creativity, and moral superiority. Disconnected from God's graceful interdependence, we drop our coins into the offering plate and, like the wealthy worshiper Jesus observed in the temple, we thank God for *our* superiority, *our* piety, and *our* faith. We discount the "widow's mite" of our poorer relations and the repentance of those whose wayward steps have led them back to church. Every faithful worship service is eucharistic, whether or not we celebrate communion weekly. In worship we recognize that all we hold most dear—life, family, nation, health, faith itself—is the gift of God within the loving, intricate, and holy web of life within which we "live and move and have our being."

In worship we celebrate the faithfulness of God in providing for our deepest needs. As such, worship is a profound act of faithful receptivity and daring trust, especially when the congregation lives financially from week to week. Still, even struggling congregations can come to recognize the grace that provides, sustains, and inspires. Week by week, small congregations, living with uncertainty, can still sing hymns like "Great Is Thy Faithfulness" and the Doxology as affirmations of God's daily providential care. When small congregations trust the truths affirmed in the hymns they sing, their spirits are transformed. Even if their faith is not manifest in numerical growth, they discover anew God's companionship, care, and inspiration.

Small congregations know what it's like to live on the edge. They struggle for survival, often in rural areas, downtown communities, or small towns; often in changing and depressed communities, abandoned by merchants, factory owners, and their own children; and often uncertain about the decade ahead. Yet in small congregations everywhere, people give thanks for simple things—the birth of a child, someone's recovery from surgery, a new member, a child's graduation, a member's new job at a local factory after months of unemployment, a life well lived and now committed to God's everlasting adventure. Like those whom Jesus describes as "blessed" in Matthew 5, small congregations have few safety nets to insulate them from the uncertainty of the future. Small congregations know that their growth and survival depend on the grace of God working within their own graceful care for one another.

As Bruce writes this chapter, he still sees the signs of yesterday's Thanksgiving dinner in the dining room adjacent to his study. The two of us, Daryl and Bruce, have both lived through a challenging year—two cases of cancer in Bruce's family and a debilitating and mysterious illness in Daryl's family—and like most Americans, we have directly experienced the impact of the economic crisis in shrinking retirement plans and investment portfolios. We have been pushed to the edge of our endurance and know firsthand that we have the creativity and perseverance to write this book only because God's gentle providence has given, and continues to give, strength, inspiration, and courage in facing our family's and the nation's challenges. Our gratitude for the graces we've received over the past year is mirrored in thousands of small congregations for whom Sunday's worship is an affirmation that God's goodness flows through our lives, sustaining, maintaining, and inspiring us. With grateful hearts we affirm:

> Now thank we all our God with heart and hands and voices,
> who wondrous things has done, in whom the world rejoices,
> who, from our mother's arms, has blessed us on our way
> with countless gifts of love, and still is ours today.[7]

TRANSFORMING PRAISE

One of Bruce's most meaningful worship experiences took place several years ago at the Wesley Theological Seminary Chapel. The occasion was the installation of Sue Zabel as full professor at the seminary. What made the occasion unique was that Professor Zabel had been recently diagnosed with cancer and would soon go on administrative leave. The service concluded with Professor Zabel's leading the congregation in Al Carmines's "God of Change and Glory." There were few dry eyes in worship as she led the hymn's refrain, "For the Giver, for the gifts, praise, praise, praise!"[8]

Vital, life-transforming worship seamlessly joins glory, gratitude, praise, and mission. Praise reflects our awareness of God's abundant blessings for ourselves and all creation. Praise inspires us to move from affirmation to generosity, knowing that all good gifts reflect God's presence in our lives and the world. At thousands of small congregations in North America, congregants stand and sing, as the offering is brought forward, words inspired by Psalm 100:

> Praise God, from whom all blessings flow;
> Praise God, all creatures here below;
> Praise God above, ye heavenly host;
> Praise Father, Son, and Holy Ghost.[9]

Praise affirms the dynamic process of giving and receiving that characterizes our relationship with God. God calls and we respond; God inspires and we create; God guides and we venture forth. Praise is our gift to God, grounded in God's gifts to us. In acts of praise, we "bless" God with all our hearts and minds. We return to God, the giver of life and love, the bounties of our own creativity. In praise, we do something beautiful for God, presenting the gifts of our lives to the One whose love brings forth spinning galaxies and crying infants.

WORSHIP AS MISSION

The signpost of a Central Pennsylvania congregation proclaims, "Enter to Worship, Go Forth to Serve." This same spirit characterizes Saturday-evening worship at Disciples United Community Church in Lancaster. Following the celebration of communion and moments of sharing life events such as birthdays and anniversaries, the congregation turns toward the door for the benediction, as a symbol of the dynamic interdependence of worship and mission. Worship transforms our vision of reality by placing God at the center of life as the source of inspiration, healing, and reconciliation. In worship, we tune our hearts toward God's voice among the many voices of life. We align ourselves with God's will for ourselves and all creation, and claim our role as God's companions in healing creation in the world beyond the church doors.

Worship joins us with our brothers and sisters in the body of Christ as a prelude to our going out into the world to share the gospel in acts of testimony, hospitality, healing, and justice making. In the wake of their dramatic experience of God's Spirit at Pentecost, the followers of Jesus gathered for worship in the emerging Jerusalem church. As they "devoted themselves to the apostles' teaching and fellowship, to the breaking of bread and the prayers . . . they would sell their possessions and goods and distribute to all as they had need" (Acts 2:42, 44). Having heard the good news, we must—as Peter discovered—widen the scope of community to include those we might previously called "unclean" or placed outside our circle of care (Acts 10).

Small churches become lights in their communities when they recognize that their participating in word, song, and sacrament nourishes them for their role as Christ's messengers to the world. The faith we affirm and the hymns and songs we sing are intended to shape the whole of our lives, not just the Sunday worship experience. With Esther, we are called for "just such a time as this." We recognize that when small congregations compare themselves to large and growing congregations, they may often feel marginalized, unimportant, and impotent. But we also affirm that they can transform their immediate communities by Christlike acts of personal and communal sharing and inclusion.

Small churches have a great impact on their communities and the world around them when their hymns and songs take wings in the commitment of a handful of junior-high students who bake brownies to raise money for the Heifer Project; when communion inspires members to serve meals at the local soup kitchen; when carols challenge people to welcome the homeless at the local shelter; and when stories of Jesus's welcoming outcasts can invite congregations to open their doors to their own community's outcasts and to break barriers of class, ethnicity, lifestyle, and sexual orientation. Seldom do such congregations make partisan political declarations, but their witness is just as effective when it joins theology, worship, and welcome.

Worship is life-changing and world-shaping. What we do in worship really matters—not just to ourselves but also to our neighborhoods. Our worship also matters to God! Blessed to be a blessing, our world expands, and small congregations discover their calling to shine the light of Christ on country roads, struggling communities, and changing neighborhoods (Matt. 5:14–16).

ENLIVENING WORSHIP AND MUSIC IN YOUR CHURCH

In this chapter's spiritual practice, worship leaders are invited to reflect on their theology of worship by considering questions such as:

1. When is God most real to you during worship?
2. What is the relationship between worship and mission?
3. In what ways does worship nurture you spiritually?

We believe that worship is connected with the totality of our lives. In the course of the week, take time to "practice worship" at home, on the job, and while running errands. Take time each day to awaken to the wonder of the world. *Pause, notice, and open yourself* to God's presence in the ordinary tasks of the day. Ponder the amazing wonder of life, whether the galaxies and solar systems or the intricately woven human body. Look for God's creative wisdom working within the world throughout the week.

In the spirit of the hymn "Now Thank We All Our God," take time throughout the week to be grateful. If you a need a few prompts, consider the following questions:

1. For what am I thankful for in my congregation?
2. For what people in my life and congregation do I give thanks?
3. As I look at my own life, for what am I most thankful?

When you are tempted to minimize the gifts of your congregation, commit yourself to saying thank you for the impact of your congregation on your life and the lives of others. Commit yourself to expressing thanks to people in your congregation for their faithful service, whether as choir singers, ushers, greeters, coffee-hour hosts, or property committee members.

Praise leads to partnership with God in the same way that worship leads to mission. God's call leads to our response. Looking at your congregation today:

1. Where do you see your congregation called to mission in the community and the wider world?
2. Where do you feel called to share God's good news in acts of kindness, service, and care?

Take some time to visualize those in your community to whom you are called to reach out. Consider ways that your congregation might be more faithful in its mission to the world.

CHAPTER 3

HOW CAN WE KEEP FROM SINGING?

TRANSFORMING MUSIC IN THE SMALL CHURCH

IN ONE OF OUR Enlivening Worship sessions at Lancaster Theological Seminary, we asked the participants to describe worship in their church. They responded with such words as *routine, traditional, predictable, meaningful, habitual, stagnant, inviting,* and *inspiring.* "What makes your worship that way?" we asked. The majority of the answers had to do with the style of music in the worship service. Members of one church said that their worship was predictable because of the use of a traditional choir, the order of the service, the use of solely piano and organ for accompanying the assembly's song, and the practice of singing from a traditional hymnbook.

Music certainly is one of the greatest gifts we have for expressing our faith and love for God. Music has a power that often the spoken word alone cannot match. Hymn writer and musician Brian Wren in his book *Praying Twice* states, "Congregational song should do something meaningful, something that makes a difference, something that moves us from one state of being to another."[1] According to Wren, music in worship should aim to be one or more of the following:

+ *Formative,* shaping and modeling our faith as it tells a story

- *Transformative*, moving us from isolation to belonging, indifference to interest, interest to conviction, and conviction to commitment
- *Cognitive*, giving us something to ponder and think about
- *Educational*, teaching us something we didn't know about the Bible, the church, and Christian faith
- *Inspirational*, lifting us out of ourselves into hope, joy, and peace[2]

When worship leaders aim at one or more of these goals, music becomes a powerful tool for life-changing worship.

Most participants in the Enlivening Worship seminars agreed that music is the one aspect often neglected in the small church. The pastors concurred that virtually no emphasis was placed on music in their seminary training. They received a wealth of information in theology, biblical interpretation, church history, clinical pastoral education, pastoral care, preaching, worship, world religions, church, and culture, but little if any training in church music. Most said that instruction in church music was not a required part of the curriculum.

Members of small churches often become depressed when they compare themselves to larger churches. They believe that their financial situation prevents them from having vital worship. Their inferiority complex is understandable.

We know a large church in our community that has money to hire a full-time musician with advanced music degrees to conduct the church's five vocal choirs and two handbell choirs in addition to playing a thirty-eight-rank pipe organ. This congregation also has the resources to hire a part-time musician to lead a praise band. The church has purchased a huge sound system and instruments to support the band. It budgets four thousand dollars a year to purchase music to add to an already enormous music library.

We often hear church leaders say that to enable the church to grow, they need to offer multiple styles of worship and music to appeal to a wide spectrum of tastes. Daryl's daughter attended a church in Southern California that offered a smorgasbord of Sunday worship services. At 8:30, there was a contemplative service; at 9:30, a classic service; at 11:00, both a contemporary service in the main sanctuary and a "seeker service" at a local nightclub down the street. On its website, this church states that its mission is to provide the congregation with a variety of worship services to meet the needs of the various constituencies within the community.

One of the key principles of this book is the affirmation that small churches do not have to stay stuck with an inferiority complex. They can have music that is spirited and meaningful. They do not need a huge budget, a big pipe organ, a multiple-choir program, or even a praise band to have faithful and vital worship. They do not need to jump on the latest trend of worship styles or use cute labels to describe their worship just to get people through the door. Small churches must, however, deliberately find ways of enlivening their worship with communal song.

While teaching a course at Lancaster Seminary titled "The Pastor and the Church Musician: Friend, Foe, or Fiasco," Daryl heard an unfortunate story. Bill was serving two small churches in rural Maryland. At one of the churches was a longtime member who had served as organist for more than fifty years. Pastor Bill loved Mary and felt indebted to her for her years of service to the church. She played her limited repertoire of hymns—all rather slowly and methodically. Mary made lots of mistakes and said she could not learn new songs. So they used the same ten to twelve songs Sunday after Sunday and year after year. Pastor Bill acknowledged that her leadership had a negative impact on worship. He found himself looking for ways to exclude her from playing too much. Daryl asked if he could recommend that she take lessons or go to seminars or workshops to help with her musical skills, but Pastor Bill felt he could not ask her to change. She was a pillar of the church and had served long and faithfully. He admitted that the church was stuck and that it could not have energetic music and worship because of her presence. Time after time, we hear stories like this. Church leaders throw up their hands and are willing to stay stuck because *that is just the way it is.*

It is a challenge to look for new ways to bring life to our worship through the gift of music. But the time is now for church leaders to break down the walls of stylistic labels and to find new ways of breathing life into worship through music. We must be determined to help people express themselves through song. To begin our journey on the path of faithful and dynamic worship, we must first look to two very fundamental aspects of the communal song: *Why do we sing in worship?* and *What do we sing in worship?*

WHY DO WE SING IN WORSHIP?

Whether your congregation is large or small, singing is at the heart of Christian worship. Singing shapes congregational life in several ways.

1. Singing builds community.

When Christians gather to worship in Zimbabwe, the service may actually begin at the edge of the village with a celebrative procession. As the worshipers gather, they may join the festivity by singing a song like "*Uyai Mose*" ("Come, All You People").[3] Each person may add his or her unique gift by dancing, stomping, clapping, hitting sticks together, playing a drum, shaking a seed-filled gourd, or improvising with the voice. As more and more worshipers gather, the song *heats up* to form a rich polyrhythmic texture. Each worshiper brings a unique, colorful thread to worship. When all the threads are woven together, a beautiful tapestry is formed. The individual threads find their true beauty only when they are joined with other threads.

Daryl finds joy when he worships God by playing a *djembe* drum on his back deck.[4] Daryl is alone, playing his own rhythms amid God's beautiful handiwork. His worship, however, is deeply enriched when he joins his brothers and sisters in a drum circle or a communal song. We each bring our own rhythm or unique vocal quality to worship. We listen to each other, we respond to what we hear, and a beautiful gift is offered. The songs we sing in worship have great power to build community.

When teaching an African song like *"Uyai Mose"* at workshops or even at St. Peter's United Church of Christ, Daryl often tells the story of the celebrative processional and the community building that happens. Daryl divides the assembly into three or four groups and gives each group a different rhythm pattern to experience. When Daryl and the congregation put the patterns together, the assembly experiences the polyrhythmic effect that comes so naturally to worshipers in Africa. We may stomp, clap, *patschen* (hit our lap with our hands), or do finger taps. Once the rhythms are produced by the body sounds, we often add instruments to the texture.

The two of us invite you to try a community-building experience by teaching your congregation these simple rhythms to a song like *"Uyai Mose."*

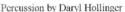

Percussion by Daryl Hollinger

Percussion Copyright © 2008 by Daryl Hollinger

2. Singing has the power to connect us with the universal church.

When we sing global songs in worship, we are connected with our brothers and sisters in other lands. Singing *"Uyai Mose"* reminds us of the extreme hardship Christians are facing in Zimbabwe, a country plagued by HIV/AIDS. The average life span of a male is thirty-seven and of a female, thirty-four. Over one-quarter of the population are refugees as a result of the harsh political and economic environment. When we sing this song, we are jolted to look beyond our safe and sheltered world. We realize that we are part of a larger family where many members suffer. The very least we can do as Christians is to pray for those who suffer as we sing the song. Perhaps we as individuals or as a congregation will be moved to further action by giving money, writing a letter to the newspaper editor, or contacting a political leader. Singing songs from other lands is a powerful tool to connect us to the wider church.

Singing may also connect us with Christians who have journeyed before us. When we sing a song like "Now Thank We All Our God," we understand how music has been a vital tool in helping believers in the past live out their faith. Martin Rinkart (1586–1649) composed this hymn as a table blessing for his family during the atrocities of the Thirty Years War. As the lone pastor in the walled town of Eilenburg, Saxony, he experienced firsthand the ravages of war as he often buried forty or fifty people in one day.[5] When Daryl tells this story before the song is sung in worship, people often tell him after the service how they were moved by hearing of the faith of Martin Rinkart. Sometimes they proceed to tell their own life story and their own hardships. The song becomes a powerful tool to encourage us on our pilgrimage. When we sing old songs, we are reminded that we belong to a great heritage of saints who have gone before us. Our faith is certainly inspired by their witness.

3. Singing hymns of faith tells the story of God's faithfulness in challenging times.

Through a song, Miriam and Moses tell the story of God's protection and deliverance of the Hebrew people (Exod. 15:1–21). They were confronted with an insurmountable obstacle as the Egyptian army chased them toward the Red Sea. A dead-end street was just ahead, and it seemed as though they had no way to turn. They were minutes from death, and God miraculously intervened by parting the sea, so that they could proceed on dry land. God's protection did not end there as the waters rolled over their enemies. It was important to the Hebrew people to retell their story through song to remind future generations of God's faithfulness.

African Americans often find an affinity with the history of the Hebrew people. Songs of both jubilation and sorrow helped slaves and their children live out their faith while enduring bondage and oppression. When we sing spirituals like "Go Down, Moses," we are given hope and courage to face what seem to be huge roadblocks in our lives. Singing their stories encourages us to remember God's faithfulness.

To capture the extreme emotion of this sorrow song, it helps to see it in the context of African American singing. Freedom in the way we sing is important in experiencing what this hymn meant to those who sang it first. Accordingly, Daryl encourages congregations to put down their hymnbooks and sing from the heart. A call and response between soloist and assembly enables the congregation to feel the spirit of the song.

> ONE: When Israel was in Egypt's Land,
> ALL: *Let my people go,*
> ONE: Oppressed so hard they could not stand,
> ALL: *Let my people go.*
> ONE: Go down, Moses; way down in Egypt's land,
> > Tell old Pharaoh,
> ALL: *Let my people go.*

The leader should encourage singers to sing freely and with emotion. Vocal slides, bending pitches, additional notes and words, and flexible rhythm will help singers identify with the pain and sorrow expressed by the song. A sense of timelessness may be achieved by repeating and adding stanzas. To truly enter into the emotion, do not be restricted to singing three or four stanzas. Let the spirit soar to new depths of feeling pain, anguish, and sorrow. By singing the song of the oppressed, we are moved to action in promoting social justice, providing hope to the marginalized, and bringing peace to a war-torn world.

4. Singing enhances the words we use in worship.

When Daryl recently presented a workshop on Lenten worship, he had the group repeat phrases after him. Trying to create an atmosphere of stillness and receptivity to meeting God in worship, Daryl spoke slowly and calmly. The group did well in following his inflections and interpretation of these words.

> We gather here—in the stillness of the hour.
> We gather here—to walk the inward way.
> Come, meet our Savior here.

Then, instead of reading the words, Daryl sang a line and the group repeated it after him. (See music in appendix B, page 199.) He played a simple accompaniment on the Celtic harp, and some worshipers played rain sticks and wind chimes. Suddenly these words were transformed.

Many remarked that the music helped them experience calm and stillness that the words alone could not provide. The slow, pensive melody was a vehicle for the worshiper to go deeper in reflecting on the inward journey of Lent. The musical interludes with harp, rain sticks, and wind chimes created a soundscape that called the worshipers to meet the Savior. The deep breathing required for singing the song helped people in the congregation to relax their bodies, which in turn helped them to clear their minds to allow space to listen to God.

No matter what style or mood is conveyed, well-crafted songs take us to a more thorough understanding of the text we are singing. All the elements of a song—the melody, rhythm, harmony, texture, timbre, and form—work together to help us engage with the text. Composers use these elements to reflect the meaning of the words. *Word painting*, the musical picto-rialization of words from the text as an expressive device, has been a common technique of songwriters since as early as the Renaissance.[6] For example, as noted musicologists Kristine Forney and Joseph Machlis suggest, "An unexpected, harsh dis-sonance might coincide with the word 'death,' or an ascending line might lead up to the word 'heavens' or 'stars.'"[7] Worshipers respond both intellectually and emotionally to this integration of text and music. While they may not be able to articulate fully the depth at which the song shapes their worship, worshipers certainly respond to the text more intensely because of the music.

5. Singing hymns of faith can provide comfort.

At Daryl's church last year, the congregation sang "Be Still and Know"[8] throughout the Lenten season. The cantor led the singing one phrase at a time, so the worshipers did not have to look at the words or the music. To enhance the experience of God's comfort to us, they used the gentle sounds of the rain stick and projected peaceful images of nature on the wall. Over the weeks, this song from Psalm 42 became a mantra of hope for many as they faced extreme hardships in their lives.

That summer Daryl's wife, Bonnie, who is pastor of his church, developed some serious health issues. The doctors put her through a myriad of tests to determine the cause of this strange and immobilizing sickness. Her hospital stay stretched from days to weeks as her condition worsened without a diagnosis.

Day after day Daryl sat by her bedside and watched helplessly as many times she was too ill to respond. Every day the sound of his brothers and sisters singing "Be Still" went through his head. Many times Daryl sang the comforting song by her bedside. There was nothing left for him to do but let that song be a vehicle to bring hope and healing. While Daryl sang Psalm 42, he knew that his brothers and sisters at St. Peter's were also praying and singing it on his family's behalf. The power of that song to keep the community's faith strong throughout those three months of the illness was beyond imagination. The members dug deep within themselves to keep their faith and church going during the absence of their pastor.

The mysterious illness left as quickly as it had come. Bonnie now has been completely healed from the infirmity. During this distressing time, however, Daryl and Bonnie were blessed by the healing power of this simple song, which brought comfort to this community of faith.

6. Singing can bring us hope.

As we sing songs that reflect the faith of both those gone before us and those living, we gain a renewed sense that God brings us hope in our faith journey. Browse through the topical index of your hymnal, and note the wide array of songs that reflect hope. In the 1989 *United Methodist Hymnal* alone, there are seventy-nine examples. Listed in this index is the song "We Shall Overcome," which was used as a powerful tool to bring hope during the civil rights struggles of the 1950s and 1960s. As people marched hand in hand singing this song, hope was implanted in those who were victims of harsh discrimination. In 1963 during the march on Washington, folk singer Joan Baez led a group of three hundred thousand in singing this song of hope in front of the Lincoln Memorial. In 1968 Martin Luther King Jr. referred to the hope of "We Shall Overcome" in his final speech before he was assassinated. The power of this song to bring hope is felt across the world—from the tobacco workers in the 1940s in South Carolina, to the Northern Ireland Civil Rights Association, to the South Africa antiapartheid movement and the Velvet Revolution in Prague, Czechoslovakia, in 1989. These are astonishing stories about the intense power of the people's song to bring hope in the direst human conditions.

7. Singing can function as a prophetic voice.

Early in Daryl's ministry at St. Peter's United Church of Christ, he taught the congregation "The Servant Song."[9] The song became a favorite of many as the simple melody and profound text became ingrained in hearts and minds. The words reflected the prophet Micah's challenge to live a life of fairness and justice and to walk humbly with God (Micah 6:8). Little did Daryl know at that time how this song would challenge the congregation to action.

That autumn Pastor Bonnie received a call from the local director of the refugee and relief agency Church World Service. Her tone was urgent as she told Pastor Bonnie about a Burmese family that had just arrived from a refugee camp in Thailand. The sponsorship for this family had just fallen through, and she was desperate for help. "Can you do anything for them?" she asked. "They are your neighbors, just a few houses down the street from your church. The couple has no money or clothing, and they have a six-month-old baby boy." Pastor Bonnie paused and took a deep breath. In her head she heard the sound of her flock singing "The Servant Song." Quickly she responded, "Sure, St. Peter's will help. When someone in need is at our doorstep, we must respond."

E-mails flew around the congregation. That Sunday the congregation was planning an outdoor service and picnic at a local park. Congregants swiftly made plans to have a shower for their new neighbors. People rallied around the cause, buying food, clothing, blankets, a stroller, and a car seat.

St. Peter's continued to support the family over the next year by helping them financially and physically to adapt to a new culture and way of life. Soon relatives joined the family in Lancaster. St. Peter's started to offer life-skills and English classes. The word spread speedily to the refugee community that there was a loving and caring group of people at the corner of College Avenue and Buchanan Avenue. St. Peter's goal was to become a place where generosity abounds unconditionally.

Today the message of "The Servant Song" is faithfully lived out by this small assembly of believers. Members of St. Peter's now offer classes every day of the week in English, life skills, and the challenge of adapting to life in the United States. Community members are capturing the vision, helping refugees from Iraq, Nepal, Thailand, Somalia, and Bhutan experience God's love. They are experiencing the joy of answering the prophet's call *to do justice, love kindness, and walk humbly with your God.*

REFLECTION

When Daryl gives workshops on why we sing in worship, he asks participants to add their own responses to the question "Why do we sing in worship?" Every congregation has its own unique reasons for singing in the assembly. We encourage small congregations to reflect on the importance of using this God-given gift. When we affirm all the wonderful benefits of singing together, we open ourselves for the Spirit to do unimaginable work within our community. Here we see the great power of the people's song to bring about life-changing worship.

WHAT DO WE SING IN WORSHIP?

As we continue our journey of worship renewal through communal song, it is important for us to look not only at *why we sing* but also *what we sing* in worship. In working with small churches, we affirm the following six theological insights that will enable congregations to embody their theology and piety and to go beyond the worship wars in the quest for faithful and vital worship in their own unique congregational context.

1. Songs reflect our theology.

> We have heard the joyful sound: Jesus saves! Jesus saves!
> Spread the tidings all around: Jesus saves! Jesus saves!
> Bear the news to every land, Climb the steeps and cross the
> waves;
> Onward!—'tis our Lord's command; Jesus saves! Jesus saves![10]

The words of this song resonate with the theology of the churches from our respective childhoods (Grace Fellowship, Range, Alabama; Congregational Mennonite Church, Marietta, Pennsylvania; and Community Baptist Church, King City, California). "Jesus Saves" was often sung during Sunday-morning worship, Sunday-night evangelistic services, Wednesday-night prayer meetings, missions conferences, and the annual week of revival meetings. This text showed the importance of evangelism among these communities. Most services ended with an altar call so that the congregation would not miss out on an opportunity to "win a soul for Jesus." The continual singing of this evangelistic song reinforced the importance these churches placed on the doctrine of salvation. It was key to their very existence. When Daryl looks through the topical index of the hymnal of his youth, he counts thirty-one entries under the topic "Soul Winning and Missions" and seventeen under the heading "Salvation."[11]

We think it is an important discipline for the leaders of small churches to take some time to reflect on the theologies that are close to the heart and mission of their church. Congregations need to take time to reflect on where they have been theologically, where they are now, and where God calls them to be in the future. This is a good time to review and study the statement of faith or creeds that a congregation uses in worship.

After a thorough discernment of your congregation's primary theologies, the next step is to make sure that your singing supports them. Take a look at the hymnal or songbook your congregation uses for worship. What topics are most well represented? Think of the topical index as a compilation of theologies available for your church to sing. Are the theologies that are dear to your heart and mission well represented in the index? If not, you may need to look for additional collections of songs to use. We suggest making a log of the songs you have used in worship over the past year. Are your congregation's principal theologies represented in your singing? It is important that we make this happen.

One of Daryl's students undertook a comparative study of a new hymnbook recently purchased by his church and the former hymnal. He was a member of an Anabaptist denomination historically known as a "peace church," in which many members were pacifists and did not participate in the military. From this study, the student discovered that the earlier hymnbook contained a section on patriotic hymns, while the new hymnal omitted such hymns. A substantial number of congregation members were upset that the patriotic hymns had been dropped. Church leaders had difficulty navigating these waters. For years, they had maintained their strong peace position while singing songs that said otherwise. Earlier leaders had not taken the time to discuss the theology of the hymns they sang. Patterns were set without much thought about singing songs that contradicted their historical theological affirmations.

Far too often songs are chosen without much thought about the meaning of the text. Continual review of your statement of faith, creeds, and current theologies in preaching and Christian education will help you discern a major portion of the repertoire of songs you need to be singing. Keep the log of songs sung in worship current, making sure that your primary theologies are well represented.

At St. Peter's, for example, the commitment to peace and justice is at the heart of the congregation's theology. We make sure that songs like "The Servant Song," "Let Justice Flow like Streams," and "You Are the Salt for the Earth, O People" are staples for our singing community. At Disciples United Community Church, the affirmation of God's presence in the practices of healing, hospitality, and social justice is central to the congregation's theology. This conviction is reflected in songs like "We Are Marching in the Light of God," "Let Us Talents and Tongues Employ," "God of Grace and God of Glory," and "Breathe on Us, Breath of God."

2. Songs reflect our piety.

In addition to choosing music that reflects our theology, it is important to think about using songs that represent our piety. Congregational musicians Linda Clark, Joanne Swenson, and Mark Stamm define *piety* as "the corporate inner life of the church, made visible in its worship, fellowship, and mission."[12] According to Perkins School of Theology worship professor Michael Hawn, "a congregation's style is an outward manifestation of its piety."[13] Do the songs we sing support the mission of our church? How we live out our faith in community needs to be affirmed in the songs we sing. This is a good time for the pastor and worship leaders to review and study the mission statement of your church.

It is also important to understand our congregational mission in the past and present, and the direction it might take in the future. Looking through archival material and talking to some older members will help us grasp the church's piety from the past. Reviewing the church's newsletter and denominational publications from the past few years will help assess how our church is living out our piety today. Visioning with the church community will help us see where our mission might take us in the future.

St. Peter's was formed in 1906 as a Sunday-school community on the campus of Lancaster Theological Seminary. It had thirty charter members and quickly grew to about 130 in 1926, when the congregation built its first building a block from the seminary. In 1954 it erected an adjacent sanctuary in response to a growing community. By 1965 the church school had grown to 260 members. In those early years an important part of the members' mission was to train children and youth to become committed disciples of Christ. Christian education of the youth was firmly supported through singing. Sharing the faith was brought out in songs like "This Little Light of Mine." Singing was an important part of expressing members' piety.

By the time Pastor Bonnie came to St. Peter's in 2004, the membership had decreased significantly. The congregation was lucky to have forty attend Sunday-morning worship, and Sunday school for children and youth was almost nonexistent. When Daryl came to St. Peter's in 2006, there was a tradition of singing "This Little Light of Mine" as a response to the Assurance of God's Grace. Pastor Bonnie came to Daryl during his first week in the parish with frustration about this song. "It sounds dreadful," she said. "There is no life; they don't sing it like they believe it; and besides, we hardly have any children attending worship. Let's do away with it." Daryl encouraged her to give it another chance. "The song certainly was a part of the church's piety over the years," Daryl noted. "Perhaps we can update the way we sing to make it relevant to where we are and where we're going."

In the following year, the members of St. Peter's were faced with some daunting questions. How do we keep this church open? Do we merge with another small church in the area? Do we close our doors? Or do we believe we still have a mission to do God's work? As the leaders prayed and wrestled with these questions, they discerned that they were going to claim God's promises and move forth boldly. As they approached the one-hundredth anniversary of the congregation's founding, they reclaimed their mission with tenacious faith. They set out on a major capital campaign to refurbish the facility. Their goal was to raise $350,000 to help make St. Peter's a welcoming and inviting place of worship. The campaign slogan was "Let's Shine."

Immediately they looked at ways to bring life to the Sunday-school song "This Little Light of Mine." The piano accompaniment took on the flavor of an animated gospel song. Before long the choir caught the fervor and began to clap along with the rhythm—just like a gospel choir. Very soon the congregation was getting into the spirit of it. Daryl recalls looking out to the congregation as he led the song. Not only were the people clapping—their faces radiated joy, excitement, and energy. They were no longer depressed. They believed they had work to do in fulfilling their mission. As a result of the campaign, they raised over four hundred thousand dollars and put in a new sound system, wheelchair-accessible restrooms, a welcoming narthex, and an elevator and air conditioning for the sanctuary. The singing of this song throughout the year helped them focus on their mission and assisted them in joyfully reclaiming their piety.

3. Songs reflect an eclectic repertoire.

In his book *Beyond the Worship Wars*, Thomas Long reflected on a study of twenty churches that he identified as having faithful and vital worship. He noted nine major characteristics these churches had in common. One of those characteristics is pertinent to our topic: *Vital and faithful congregations emphasize congregational music that is both excellent and eclectic in style and genre.*[14] (We will discuss the "excellent" portion in chapter 4.) Church leaders often come to our seminars thinking that they have basically two styles of music from which to choose: traditional and contemporary. The former typically involves hymns sung from a hymnal and with an organ or piano accompaniment. The latter most often involves singing "praise and worship" songs with the words projected on a screen and accompaniment provided by a praise band. Sometimes church leaders think the only way to enliven the worship is to add a contemporary service while maintaining a traditional service. Small churches often feel caught in a dilemma, because they do not have the resources for two services. They sometimes solve this problem by looking at a blending of the two styles in one service.

We see a major flaw in this assumption. Thinking only in terms of traditional and contemporary often sets up conditions for the eruption of worship wars. Larry came to one of Daryl's workshops and told his story. He was a part-time director of music in a small United Methodist church in a Southeastern Pennsylvania village. When he first came to the church, the singing was solely from the *United Methodist Hymnal* and was accompanied by the organ. Gradually a tiny group in the church began to ask for a contemporary service. The church board members knew they did not have the resources for two services, so they asked Larry to start adding some praise songs to the service. He gradually added several, but the group that made the initial request was not happy. People in this group said the congregation was not singing enough songs in worship that they liked. Those used to singing from the hymnal were also upset with the new style of music. The board met again and decided that 40 percent of the songs should be contemporary and 60 percent traditional. Larry kept a log of the songs the congregation sang and tried to adhere to the prescribed formula. The two camps became more and more divided, even though Larry was trying to please both. He finally resigned in frustration after two years.

Daryl suggested that Larry might want to take a new approach in his next church. When we use the words *contemporary* and *traditional*, we risk setting up a polarity. Often people have preconceived ideas about what to expect from a worship service when these terms are used. If we sing only "praise and worship" songs, we are limiting the singing of our faith to a genre that comes mostly from a thirty-year period. If we sing songs only from our hymnbook and use only organ accompaniment, we are limiting our worship by excluding many other rich traditions. By singing music from many times and places, we expand our expression of faith.

An eclectic repertoire expands our focus in such a way that we affirm both our favorite styles of music and music from the larger community of faith. When we sing an ancient chant, we reflect on the faith of those who lived before us. When we sing the songs of another land, we think about the global community of faith to which we belong. When we sing songs that are especially meaningful to the sister sitting next to us in worship, we are reminded that we belong to a local community of believers. We may like certain styles more than others, but it is important for us to sing the songs embraced by our brothers and sisters in order to fully live in community. This approach helps us move from the "I" to the "we" in worship.

Singing global songs in worship is a good way to help congregations move beyond the worship wars by opening us to the whole range of Christian music, both familiar and novel. Singing global songs reminds us that there are many kinds of Christian music, each of which reflects a particular community's faith and worship experience. Rather than being the *only* appropriate form of music, the hymns we sing and the music we plan represent only one of many possible approaches to faithful worship.

Global songs enable us to connect a bit to the life, work, celebrations, and suffering of our brothers and sisters around the world. In this way we are encouraged to pray for the world. Singing globally may be a source of welcome or hospitality to those not steeped in traditional European/North American worship. When a neighbor from Burma joins us in worship, he or she may not feel so left out if those gathered are learning a song from another land and in another tongue. Singing global songs in American churches creates a musical dialogue between the West and other parts of the world. No longer are worship and cultural elements flowing only one way, as they were in the colonization and mission work of the nineteenth century.

Finally, singing globally influences our theology. Michael Hawn suggests that the consistent use of global music opens us to new ways of understanding traditional Christian doctrines such as the incarnation, creation, the Holy Spirit, and eschatology.[15] By singing the songs from around the world, we hope to become better equipped to answer the question that Michael Hawn raises: *Is there any room for my neighbor at the table?*[16]

4. Songs honor God.

Music is a God-given gift that has many wonderful benefits. Music often brings the listener much joy and pleasure. When we learn to play or sing skillfully, our enjoyment is magnified. While these simple pleasures may happen in worship, it is important to remember that the primary object of our worship is God. Living out this conviction, however, may be difficult. For example, we may become so enthralled with a jubilant choir anthem that we spontaneously burst forth with applause. We need to look at our motives. Is the applause directed toward God, or is it saying, "Your performance of that piece was great"?

While it is important for us as leaders in small churches to offer our best gifts to God and the community of faith, we need constantly to keep our egos in check. Affirming the gifts among the community is a good and desirable trait. However, receiving those compliments must be done with graciousness, thanksgiving, and certainly not in an egotistical manner. Avoiding words like *performance* and replacing them with language like *musical offering* or *God-given gift* will help remind us that the purpose of our music is to honor God and to enliven our awareness of God's presence in our midst, and not to bolster our egos.

This concept is countercultural in our consumer-driven society, which glorifies egocentrism. How many times do we hear sayings like this: *Have it your way. It's all about you.* Or: *Be all you can be.* These cultural norms often creep into our churches today. The prosperity gospel is widespread and is manifested by teachings such as the *Prayer of Jabez*[17] or the distortion of Jesus's words "Ask and you shall receive." Looking at Jesus's life and ministry in its totality projects a much different gospel.

> Blessed are the poor in spirit, for theirs is the kingdom of heaven. . . . Love your enemies and pray for those who persecute you.
>
> —MATTHEW 5:3, 44

> Do not store up for yourselves treasures on earth where moth and rust consume.
>
> —MATTHEW 6:19

> If any want to become my followers, let them deny themselves and take up their cross and follow me.
>
> —MATTHEW 16:24

Jesus's life brought honor to God through a life of servanthood. If we adhere to the way of Jesus, our songs and music will honor not ourselves but the Creator who gave us these gifts in the first place.

Take an inventory of the songs you use in worship. Are the majority of the songs directed toward God or about God? Or do most of the songs refer to "I" or "me"? While certainly our walk with God is a personal journey, using a steady diet of "I" and "me" in our songs inclines us toward an egocentric religion. By using "we" in our songs, we remind ourselves that church is about community. When our songs direct our focus to God, we celebrate the deity who is the true object of our worship.

5. Songs support the liturgy and Scriptures of the day.

We often hear the following comments in worship workshops:

- ✦ "Pick something happy, upbeat—something that will catch their attention."
- ✦ "It doesn't matter if the hymns do not reflect the Scripture."
- ✦ "The important thing is that they are familiar so that all will enjoy them."

Statements like these by pastors or worship leaders make the communal song sound like a commodity we are trying to sell, a product people will want or like. Songs that support the liturgy and Scripture have great potential for vital worship.

By using songs that reinforce the liturgy, congregants experience a thread that connects the various components of worship. Think of using songs throughout the service to enhance the meaning and flow. Chapter 5 deals with creative ways to use music in the gathering rites, processionals, confessions, psalm singing, Scripture, sermon, prayers, offering, communion, and sending. The choir, handbell choir, percussion ensemble, and instrumentalists are important agents for enlivening the people's song.

It is also important that the hymns and songs reflect the Scripture and theme of the service. Much preparation and communication is required to do this well. Here is a twelve-step plan to assist the worship planning team in the process of selecting hymns and songs.

1. Begin by praying together.
2. Read and study the Scriptures for the day.
3. Determine the major theme of the day.
4. Ask, "Where do the hymns or songs fit into the big picture?" (Are they part of the gathering, word, meal, or sending?)

5. Consider what happens before and after the song. (Look at mood, tempo, and volume.)
6. Reflect on your congregation's history of hymn singing. (Keeping a log of songs used will help you determine which ones most congregants know and don't know.)
7. Think about your congregation's musical proficiency. (How often can the worshipers in the pews sing a new hymn? How do they best learn a new song?)
8. Keep in mind the skill level of the musical leaders and accompanists. (This approach will help determine which songs and styles are feasible options.)
9. Look for hymns and songs in indexes. (Most congregational songbooks include lectionary, scriptural, and topical indexes.
10. List several possibilities for each hymn or song slot.
11. Sing through new each hymn before including it in the service to discern its relationship with the theme and spirit of the worship service.
12. Base your hymn and song selections on these listed considerations. (Keep in mind these important aspects: How does the text match the theme and season? What mood is needed for this particular spot in the service? How singable is the song? How familiar is the song? Do we need to teach it?)

6. Songs are participatory.

If worship truly is the work of the people, our singing needs to be done in a way that encourages participation. Take a moment to observe worshipers during the singing at your church. Do the facial expressions indicate that they are connecting with the text and mood of the song? What about the body language? Do their bodies look as though they are fully participating? Is there a posture of receptiveness, or are they slouched with arms folded? We have observed many levels of participation during the singing in worship. When in our respective roles as church musician and congregational pastor, we see an obvious lack of interest or nonparticipation, we are challenged to find ways to get the worshiper actively involved.

People rationalize their lack of participation in the following ways:

- "I can't sing on pitch."
- "People tell me I have a lousy voice."
- "I feel more comfortable just listening."
- "I don't like that song."
- "This song is too hard to sing."

Whatever the reasons cited, music leaders in small churches can creatively respond to those things that block participation. Good singing in church does not just happen. The song leader must find ways to encourage the congregation to sing. Modeling with his or her voice will help the assembly hear and understand the multiple aspects of the song. Posture, facial expression, and words of introduction should be friendly and inviting. The music must be accessible to the average singer. Use songs in a comfortable range with no awkward leaps. The rhythm should be simple enough for the assembly to pick up easily. Chapter 4 will give more practical ways to draw everyone into the worship experience through the communal song.

In conclusion, our singing transforms our lives. If singing is praying twice, then we need to take our hymns seriously and understand them as ways we can open ourselves to God's presence in our lives and join our brothers and sisters in prayerful and life-transforming worship.

ENLIVENING MUSIC AND WORSHIP IN YOUR CHURCH

Find a forum for further congregational discussion of the topics *why* and *what* we sing in worship. It may take the form of a church retreat, Sunday-school forum, or even a hymn sing during worship. Try to find a time when many folk from your church will be able to attend and have a voice. Encourage participants to share other reasons it is important to sing communally in worship. Each congregation is unique and must find its own identity for singing together. We have found this approach to be an important first step in promoting faithful and vital worship through music in small congregations.

One of the main points of this chapter is the affirmation that the hymns we sing shape our lives. In the days ahead, choose a few hymns to sing throughout the day. Daryl found solace in a time of crisis by living with a simple chant, "Be Still." This chant comforted both Daryl and Bonnie as they journeyed through the valley of illness and uncertainty. After Bruce was unexpectedly "downsized" by the university where he had served as chaplain for seventeen years, his faith was nurtured by the hymn "How Can I Keep from Singing?"

Prayerfully reflect on the following question: What hymns nurture your spirit and give you a sense of God's abiding and challenging presence? Take time to let these hymns transform the way you look at God's presence in your life by using them as opportunities for prayer.

CHAPTER 4

THE WORK OF THE PEOPLE

GOOD SINGING IN THE ASSEMBLY

Now THAT WE HAVE discussed *why* and *what* we sing in worship, it is important for us to look at the *how*. To be faithful in our worship to God, we need to give our best gifts. This includes the gift of music and does not depend on professionals or piped-in music to be excellent. Even in a small church good singing is paramount and achievable.

There are many reasons why poor singing is evident in churches. Brian Wren notes several reasons why congregational song is in trouble:

1. Individualism . . . makes us less inclined to join a group and sing along.
2. Popular music is soloistic.
3. Live music is no longer the norm, so our role as listeners is reinforced.
4. The quality of recorded sound persuades us that our own voice has little value.
5. High amplification . . . overwhelms the communal voice and discourages participation.
6. We have no folk or community repertoire.[1]

Even though these reasons may all be valid and prevalent, there is no need to stay stuck. Small churches may find this a particularly difficult challenge, but we assert that congregational singing can be enriched by techniques that are simple and will assist the congregation in creating excellent music.

Pastor Roberts came to our worship workshop rather discouraged by the lack of congregational participation in singing at his church. "I'm not sure anyone can sing at all," he said. "The organist plays every hymn the same way and often so loudly that none of us can hear each other." Pastor Roberts went on to say that the hymns chosen varied little in style and rarely appealed to the youth or children. He was not advocating a new hymnal but said he wished there was a way the congregation's singing could gain some life to more fully inspire the praise of God.

Pastor Roberts participated in the Enlivening Worship seminar, and through the use of techniques he learned at the event, he was able to bring about some significant changes in his congregation's singing. These are the six characteristics of good singing in the assembly that we taught him and others.

1. Good leadership draws everyone into worship.

It takes a strong and engaging leader to draw everyone into singing. We recommend that musicians frequently lead in front of the assembly. This may mean getting off the organ or piano bench and facing the congregation. A good leader can do many things to enhance singing. The obvious role of the song leader is to get the assembly to begin together, stay together, and end together. However, much more needs to happen. Enthusiasm is exhibited when the leader brings the text of the song to life. The posture, body language, and facial expressions of the song leader should reflect the meaning and emotion of the song. When a leader is involved in this manner, participants are encouraged to join in at a deeper level.

The songs chosen for singing must be accessible to the average singer. This means that a song must be within the musical

range of most singers. Daryl recommends this range for congregational singing.

Congregations sing better in the middle part of the range.
Songs that stay for some time at the extremes of the range will
be difficult for many singers. Beginning a song with a high note
or a low note does not work well. Songs are easily sung when
they move primarily by scale step with intermittent skips. The
skips must not be large or difficult to sing. We suggest that congregations generally avoid using songs with awkward skips like
the augmented fourth or the major seventh.

Take a look at the contemporary song "On Eagle's Wings."[2]
Although the text is meaningful, certain aspects of the song
make it difficult to sing. The opening note begins on a C#6,
which is in the extreme high range. The note is also the seventh of the chord. Both these factors make the song difficult
for a small congregation to sing well. There are ways of getting
around this problematic portion of the song. While we affirm
the theology reflected in "On Eagle's Wings," we recommend
letting a soloist or choir sing the stanzas, the most difficult portion, and having the assembly sing the easier refrain.

Rhythm is another aspect of congregational music that requires a discriminating leader. We recommend using songs in
which the rhythm reflects the natural stress and flow of the text.
More important words need to have more stress than less important words. Certain syllables of words also have a natural
stress while other syllables require less stress. A general rule to
follow is that the most important words and syllables should fall
on beat 1 of a measure (immediately after the bar line). Secondary accents fall on beat 2 in 4/4 time and on beat 4 in 6/8. Take
a look at the opening phrase of the hymn "Guide Me, O Thou

Great Jehovah." The words or syllables *guide, great, pil-(grim)*, and *bar-(ren)* naturally receive more stress when spoken. Therefore they fall on beat one. Secondary accents are on the word/syllables O, *(Je)ho-(vah), through,* and *land*, and fall on beat 3.

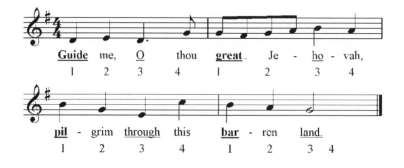

When the music does not reflect the natural accent of the text, the song sounds forced and is difficult to sing. Daryl wrote the following example to show how awkward singing is when the music does not match the natural accent of the text. Notice the emphasis on the less significant words or syllables, which fall on the strong beats. Even though the tune is catchy, the text and music don't enhance one another.

Syncopation, the temporary shifting of the accent to a weaker beat, is a characteristic of gospel and contemporary songs. When used sparingly in congregations unfamiliar with gospel music, this technique helps add vitality to the singing of some songs. Complicated syncopated patterns, however, are difficult for many congregations to maneuver. This song involves simple syncopated rhythms and is fairly easy for a small congregation to sing,

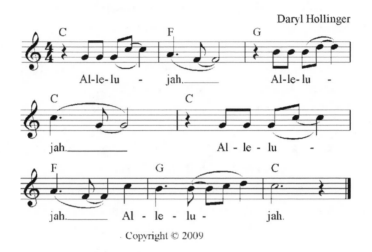

Daryl Hollinger

Copyright © 2009

In contrast, the excerpt below has complex syncopated rhythms and would be tricky for an assembly to sing. While music like this may be great for a praise band or soloist, congregations will have a hard time keeping it together.

Daryl Hollinger

Copyright © 2009

Leaders need discernment to select songs that are easy for the assembly to sing. Often worship planners neglect this important aspect of helping the congregation to sing well. The fact that a song or hymn is published in a book does not mean that it is easy for your assembly to sing. When the song is difficult to sing, the congregation is quickly discouraged and many may sing halfheartedly or even stop singing altogether.

Contemporary songs are often a challenge for congregations to sing as well. Sometimes these songs are inaccessible for congregations because of the nature of the music. They often are soloistic, contain unpredictable harmonic changes, have melodies that are difficult to sing, and make use of complicated rhythms. When churches use a song from a recording artist, the music often does not work well because it is designed for professionals and not for communal singing.

This genre can be vital to worship, however, when care is taken to choose songs that are accessible to the assembly. Terri McClean, award-winning songwriter and contemporary-worship leader, recommends a four-filter process for determining which contemporary songs will work well for your congregation.[3] One filter deals extensively with choosing music that is easy to sing. In our Enlivening Worship seminars, we recommend that musicians help the worship planning team work through this filter. The leaders who participated in our seminar and used these filters experienced excellent results.

2. Good singing is modeled by the human voice.

Daryl begins this portion of his workshop by leading the assembly in singing the spiritual "Go Down, Moses" without using any printed music. He first sings the phrase "Let my people go" in a somber and covered tone. He leans on the word *let*, uses a dark "ah" vowel on *my*, and slides into the word *go*. Then he asks the people to sing the phrase just as they heard it. Without his offering any explanation or using technical terms, the assembly is quickly able to sing and convey the deep emotion of this spiritual. These intricate nuances of singing are difficult to explain. Modeling them with the human voice, however, is simple. (The rest of the song may be sung following the call-and-response procedure outlined in chapter 3.)

If we introduce a song only by playing it on an instrument, the congregation will have very little information about how to sing it. Although congregants will catch the tempo, pitches, rhythm, and perhaps a bit of the mood of the song from an instrumental introduction, they will often have no clue about the vocal color, diction, vowels, accent, and the array of emotion that the voice can express. A great deal of information, meaning, and emotion can be achieved in congregational singing when the leader models the singing with his or her voice.

The music leader must exhibit confidence as well as skill in projecting all these qualities to the assembly. Daryl often coaches organists or pianists to help them feel comfortable in this role. This does not mean that the leader must be an opera singer. In fact, a small congregation will respond more readily to a warm, folk-singing voice than to a big, operatic voice. The leader, however, must learn good vocal techniques, including diaphragmatic breathing, diction, pure vowel production, and projection. Some vocal lessons may help the leader gain confidence in this area.

When a leader is ready to lead with his or her voice, careful thought should be given to how the song will be modeled. One may choose to "line out" a song one phrase at a time. This was the common practice in early American churches for teaching a song in the absence of accompaniment or a hymnal. The *Vorsänger* or *Praecentor*, or song leader, would sing one line, and the congregation would repeat it. The rest of the hymn was sung in this manner, one phrase at a time. Alice Parker, well-respected composer, arranger, and enlivener of congregational song, states that the "cantor alone can best work in phrases. A phrase is a *memorable unit*—anything longer is too much to remember."[4] Some leaders may choose to sing a single stanza or refrain to help worshipers learn a song. Many details of the song may be taught in this manner, but if the song is too long or complicated, the assembly will not be able to remember all the parts of the song.

The leader needs to spend time studying the song before jumping in and leading it. Careful thought should be given to interpreting the song. What is the mood of the text and music? What vocal quality best depicts this mood? Try to define it with adjectives like *bright*, *dark*, *covered*, *thin*, *heavy*, or *warm*. Where are the important words? Where do we breathe? What volume and tempo best express the meaning of the song? Daryl recommends that the song leader mark his or her score indicating tempo, dynamics, stress (accented and unaccented notes), color of vowels, phrasing, and so forth. After determining how to sing the song, the leader must practice the song, so that he or she can sing it with ease. All these details must be learned well before one tries to teach them to the assembly. When the leader memorizes the specific song, he or she is able to connect with the singers by using eye contact, facial expression, body movement, or hand gestures.

Confidence is gained by practicing and leading. A leader should not think that he or she has to be perfect in leading with the voice. Practice by teaching the song to the choir before teaching it to the entire assembly. We suggest asking the choir what worked and what didn't. Just like anything else, this method becomes easier with practice. We advise that you take time after leading the song to reflect on how it went by asking such questions as: What could you do differently? How could you make it easier for the assembly to learn? No matter what, do not give up on modeling with your voice. Not every song will be appropriate to learn in this way. Teaching by modeling with the voice on various occasions will greatly enhance the quality of singing in your church, however. It is well worth the effort.

3. Good singing is enhanced by proper breathing.

Learning to breathe correctly is the most fundamental aspect of good singing. Most vocal coaches teach proper breathing techniques in the very first lesson. Breathing correctly is a natural physical activity that we all do from infancy. Somehow, as we grow up, many of us start to take on bad habits. When Daryl asks untrained singers to take a big breath, he often observes the singers attempting to do strenuous contortions with the body. Frequently he notices heaving in the chest and tension in the neck and face.

Correct breathing is an uncomplicated concept involving the diaphragm, a muscle right below the lungs and above the vital organs. When the diaphragm is relaxed, it is in the shape of an upside-down bowl. Upon inhalation, the lungs fill up with oxygen, which flattens the diaphragm, thus causing the stomach area to expand.

Take some time to watch a baby breathe. You will notice that the only movement is from the stomach, not the chest, neck, or face. As the baby inhales, the tummy expands. As he or she exhales, the tummy goes in. Singing involves this effortless movement. You may try a simple exercise to demonstrate the process. Lie flat on your back—hands by your side. Place a book on your stomach and slowly inhale through the nose. As you do, you should notice the book start to rise. There is no movement from anywhere except the stomach. When you have fully inhaled, pause and slowly let the air out with a hissing sound. Make a slow and steady air stream as you exhale. Notice that the book now goes slowly back down. Practice this technique until it feels natural to you and your air stream is controlled. You have just completed the correct technique for singing. Instead of hissing, of course, we are singing. You can develop your breath control by practicing this technique often. By gradually increasing the amount of time you exhale on the hiss, you increase the length of time you can sing a phrase.

Obviously, you probably would not try this exercise with your congregation during a worship service. It is important, however, that the song leader understand this concept and be able to model correct breathing before the assembly. Practice modeling good posture and breath control in front of a mirror or before some friends. On the inhalation, be deliberate about

portraying a slow breath through the nose. The following hand
gesture will help the assembly know what to do before singing.
Begin with both hands about two inches in front of your stomach and parallel to the floor. Allow a two- to four-inch space
between your hands. As you breathe in, make a downward circular motion. Take the circle downward toward the navel before
moving the circle upward to shoulder level. This completes the
inhalation. Now make a firm downward motion (about four
inches) to indicate the beginning of the singing. Again, practicing these gestures in a mirror will help you see whether you are
communicating the natural inhalation technique.

Here is a worship practice that will further teach proper
breathing for singing. It is a guided meditation that may be
used as a confession or during the prayers. Feel free to adapt
the prayers to complement the season, the theme of the service,
or needs within your congregation.

> As we approach this time of prayer, I invite you to get in a
> comfortable position—back straight and eyes closed. Place
> one hand on your side, just under the ribcage. As we breathe
> in deeply, invite God's presence to be with you. When you
> feel the expansion of your stomach, imagine the very being of
> God dwelling within you. As you exhale, make a soft hissing
> sound. When you feel your stomach going in, visualize the
> junk in your life leaving your body. Slowly breathe in God's
> goodness. Now exhale what is troubling you. Breathe in . . .
> two, three, four. Exhale . . . two, three, four. Breathe in . . . two,
> three, four. Exhale . . . two, three, four.

God of peace and love, we long for serenity within our being. Yet we are plagued with the burdens of the week. We
are troubled by conflict within our families, among our loved
ones, and in the workplace. Peace and tranquility evade us.
How often do we try to achieve serenity on our own and fail
to take our troubles to you? O God, we cry to you for help.

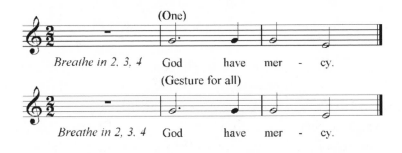

We have been so bogged down with our own junk that we
often fail to get outside ourselves to see the needs of others.
All around the world, poverty and suffering prevail. Children
are hungry and malnourished. Young girls are sold into sex
trafficking, and refugees flee their homelands to avoid being
killed. We have been so blinded by our own agenda that we
have not stopped to take notice. O God, hear our prayer.

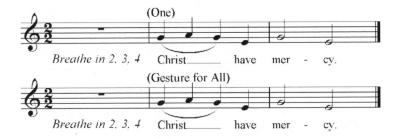

Forgive us our shortsightedness. Help us see more clearly so
that we can fulfill your mandate to take up your cross and
follow you. Give us strength and courage for the journey, and
grant us your peace.

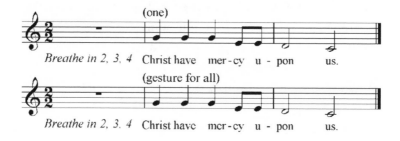

This worship practice will teach good breathing and greatly enhance the quality of singing in the assembly without your having to explain the technical details. If done prayerfully, the physical aspect of breathing and the guided images have the power to reflect God's peace and mercy in troubled times.

4. Good singing is musical.

Getting the assembly to sing in a musical manner is another goal that may be achieved by modeling with the voice. Daryl teaches musicality in his workshops by singing a song like "Of the Father's Love Begotten." He simply sings one phrase at a time and has the congregation repeat what he sang. When he sings the opening phrase, "Of the Father's love begotten," he matches the rising and falling of the musical line. He gradually increases the energy and volume as he approaches the word *love* and then decreases the volume for the rest of the phrase. He also increases the tempo slightly as the phrase progresses and then relaxes the tempo at the end of the phrase. The flexibility in tempo is referred to as *rubato*. Special care is given when adding a little stress to the important words and syllables. In the first phrase, he leans on the syllable *Fa-* of *Father* and on *got-* of *begotten*. He sings the second phrase, "ere the worlds began to be," in a similar manner, this time with a little more energy. The third phrase, "He is Alpha and Omega," is sung with even more energy as this phrase reaches a climax in the music and the text. The highest point of the song is on the word *Alpha* and therefore demands the highest intensity of the song. In the fourth phrase, he lowers the intensity by gradually singing more slowly and softly.

By going through a song in this manner, the assembly learns the basic concepts of musicianship without any technical instruction. Singing musically is easy to learn when it is modeled effectively. In this case, the assembly quickly learned that music is more than just singing one note after another in a monotonous fashion. Rather, the notes progress in a manner reflecting the natural flow of the text. The meaning of the text is greatly enhanced through the singer's use of volume, tempo, and accent.

Other songs may be taught in a similar manner. The church musician must take time to study the song and interpret the musical components that will enhance the text. The style of some songs demands different musical aesthetics. For example, it would be musically incongruent to use *tempo rubato* in a Renaissance dance. The light accents on beat 1 of the dance require the tempo to remain steady. It is, therefore, important for the musical leader to understand the traits of various song styles. Taking a little time to model musicality in the small church will bring great rewards. Indeed, the intimacy of smaller congregations will enable the gathered assembly to notice something different about the singing. Worshipers may not be able to describe it in technical terms, but they will sense that the singing has more vitality and meaning.

5. Good singing is faithful to its historical context.

Not all songs have the same musical aesthetic. How many times have you heard someone complain about the hymn singing?

"All the songs sound the same—there's no variety."

"Why does he [or she] play all the songs so slowly? Can't we have a little life?" Many church musicians play hymns in only one musical style. Often they learned to play hymns on the organ in a precise and technical manner; as a result, to many ears the hymns sound the same. They have little variation in tempo, dynamics, accents, timbre, and articulation. When a church musician studies the historical and social context in which the song was written and ties the song's historical context to the singing within the assembly, the vitality and energy are greatly improved and the assembly will gain a better understanding of the faith journey of the people who lived during that era.

Let us look at two contrasting styles of congregational song. Here are some very simple and practical tips for bringing life to a song.

Chant Music

"Of the Father's Love Begotten" is an example of medieval plainsong. This style of music was originally sung in unison. It had a flexible rhythm that reflected the natural patterns of speech. Strong accents and a feeling of pulse were nonexistent. The tone quality of the voice was light and pure and had no vibrato. Musicians often do a disservice by adding harmonization and accompaniment to chant music. It is most beautiful and meaningful when sung simply a cappella and in unison. Many hymnals supply complex organ harmonies that make it sound more like a nineteenth-century German chorale. By singing it in its original simple style, the assembly is transported to another time and place. The style reminds the worshiper of the faith of the believers who lived more than a millennium ago.

As chant music evolved in the ninth century, a second melody or countermelody a fourth or fifth away was added to the original melody. This was called *organum*. An easy way to emulate this open, hollow sound is to create a simple accompaniment to the chant based on open fifths. "O Come, O Come, Emmanuel" is a plainsong that may be easily adapted to reflect early organum. The accompaniment may be played on a soft organ stop or handbells or hand chimes, or sung on a neutral syllable by the choir. This is an excellent opportunity to introduce handbells or hand chimes in your small church. Anyone—even non–music readers—can play these hand chimes. This technique involves four people, each playing two notes. Because the music moves slowly, you may just point to the ringers when it is their time to play.

O Come, O Come, Emmanuel

Plainsong
arr. Daryl Hollinger

Copyright © 2009 by Daryl Hollinger

In the twelfth century, *florid organum* started to appear. This music contained two parts: an upper voice moving at a regular tempo and a contrasting lower voice of slow, sustained tones. Here is a simple way to sing "Of the Father's Love Begotten" to reflect this style. Give a few words of instruction to the assembly before you begin. Divide the congregation into two sides. Have the left side sing phrase 1 and hold the final note. While these singers are holding this note, have the other side sing phrase 2 and hold the final note. As the right side continues to hold the note, cue the left side to begin phrase 3. Continue singing the rest of the song in this manner. By singing the song this way, we get a little glimpse of the sound of early chant singing. Putting the hymn in this ancient context, we are reminded of the saints who have gone before us and of the universality of our faith.

RENAISSANCE/BAROQUE DANCE

Take a look at a completely different song style. "Praise to the Lord, the Almighty" (LOBE DEN HERREN) was written in 1665 at the height of the Baroque period. During this period, many of the songs sung for fun and entertainment were in a dance form. With this in mind, let's transform this song to a lively dance. Take the tempo at a lively pace, so that you feel one beat per measure. To do this effectively, you will need to simplify the accompaniment. Add some light upward arpeggios with the left hand and reduce the frequency of chord changes. Now add a tambourine and finger cymbals.

© 2009 by Daryl Hollinger

If you have a keyboard available, change the sound to an accompaniment instrument of the period (harpsichord or lute). Suddenly this hymn has been totally transformed by the addition of just a few elements from the historical context.

Most church musicians play this song as adapted by William S. Bennett in 1863. Because this nineteenth-century setting has frequent chord changes, the tempo must slow down to accommodate the harmonic rhythm. The norm for singing this hymn is the slow and robust sound of the Romantic period. While interpreting it this way may work well for a slow, majestic processional, singing in the dance style of the Baroque will breathe new energy and life to this old, familiar song. At the 2009 Penn Central Conference Annual Meeting of the United Church of Christ, this song was sung as a processional with a troupe of dancers using tambourines with attached colored streamers—a far cry from the slow, dirgelike processional often used.

By studying the historical period in which the song was written, we are better equipped to make decisions about how to sing the song. Obviously, we cannot precisely replicate the song as sung in its original context, but we can take certain characteristics from the period and put them into our singing. Understanding the context of a song helps us connect with people of faith from the past. By understanding the political and social issues of the period, we are better able to relate to the personal journeys of those gone before us.

6. Good singing in church uses an eclectic repertoire.

In chapter 3, we dealt extensively with the need to use a wide variety of songs in our worship. We presented a rationale that included the following:

- Worship is not about what we like or dislike.
- Our songs express the expansiveness of our faith.
- Global songs may be a sign of welcome.
- Diverse repertoire influences our theology.

To have good singing in worship, it is important that we apply these principles, which support an eclectic repertoire. Accordingly, we need to have a good understanding of the various styles available to us. In chapter 5, we will present an overview of some of the styles and how to incorporate them simply and creatively into your repertoire. Our goal in this and the next chapter is not to be all-inclusive, but to help worship leaders begin to think about ways of expanding the repertoire of song in your church.

Good singing is an achievable goal for small churches. Leaders will need vision to develop a strategy to make it happen. Small churches need not be stuck with the mentality that they cannot sing well because they are limited in size and resources. Alice Parker states:

> There are churches in all denominations in this country where congregations do sing well, and it is always because there is at least one person who is actively expecting it. . . . We need to rethink our training of church music leaders, with the first priority given to raising expectations about congregational singing. The congregational voice is the heart of all church music. It can and should be beautiful, meaningful, musical, full of the Spirit, responsive both to text and tune, and magnetic in drawing together all who hear.[5]

When congregational musicians make a commitment to faithful excellence in leading music and exploring new ways of singing traditional hymns, small congregations can do great things in worship.

ENLIVENING WORSHIP AND MUSIC IN YOUR CHURCH

Psalm 150:6 proclaims, "Let everything that breathes praise [God]." As we have noted in this chapter, the way we breathe is central to our worship experiences. Regular breath prayers such as the one we described earlier in this chapter can deepen not only your singing but also your experience of God. In the following exercise, begin by reciting, "Let everything that breathes praise God." Then breathe slowly and deeply from the diaphragm. With every inhaled breath, experience God's presence filling your being. As you exhale, let your praises come forth. You may choose to silently repeat a prayer such as "I praise God for _____." Some examples might be:

"I praise God for *the opportunity to worship this week.*"
"I praise God for *the love of my family.*"
"I praise God for *the gift of life.*"
"I praise God for *the strength to grow through this experience.*"
"I praise God for *new ideas and the opportunity to change my life.*"

What is most important here is that your whole life becomes an act of praise and appreciation, not only in congregational worship but throughout the week.

CHAPTER 5

SING TO GOD
A NEW SONG

DEVELOPING AN ECLECTIC REPERTOIRE

NUMEROUS TIMES throughout the Hebrew Psalter, instruction is given to sing a new song to God. Psalm 96:1–2 proclaims, "O sing to [God] a new song; sing to [God], all the earth. Sing to [God], bless [God's] name; tell of [God's] salvation from day to day." This imperative is often followed by words describing God's faithfulness or acts of mercy. The Psalms were intended to proclaim our faith in God. Today many small churches will experience God's fullness and blessings when the songs they sing are an expression of their faith. Expanding our repertoire beyond just a single genre or two and a handful of "golden oldies" enlarges beyond measure our view of God, the world, and humanity. Singing an eclectic repertoire enables us to look beyond our own little world and to experience the expansiveness of God's realm.

We encourage worship leaders to be bold in this proclamation of faith. It is not about aesthetics—about what we like or dislike. It is about singing our faith in our local community while opening ourselves to new possibilities for singing and worship. This chapter is intended to take small churches beyond what they may be accustomed to singing. Our desire is for worship teams to capture a vision of the rich possibilities of song styles and to grow in faith by singing the stories of those

79

from the past and from other parts of the world. As in the previous chapter, some of this material is technical. We recommend that church musicians work through these principles and explain their findings to the rest of the team. Simple methods will be offered to enable music leaders to enliven various song styles for congregational singing. We will present a brief overview of nine contrasting styles and some straightforward ways of putting songs into the context in which they were written. We dealt with chant music and Baroque/Renaissance dance music in chapter 4. Let us embark on an adventure of singing a new song to our God.

EARLY AMERICAN

Early American music began with the songs from the New England school of music in the last part of the eighteenth century. It spread rapidly from New England, down the eastern seaboard and into the southern states. All-day sings developed as social events for rural communities. They were a means of learning a cappella music in four parts from the shaped-note hymnals. The singers sat in their respective voice parts in a "hollow square"—sopranos facing tenors, and altos facing basses. In the middle of the square, a singer would stand and direct the chorus. The pattern was easy, so all took turns directing the singing. The director began with a clenched fist about shoulder level. Then he or she moved the arm in a swift and energetic downward motion on beat 1 of the music and returned it to the original position for beat 2. The music had just two beats portrayed by this downward and upward movement. The energy level was so intense that at many times all the singers would start conducting the beat.

The music of the American frontier exhibited a ruggedness displayed in strong accents on beat 1 and open-sounding harmonies based on the intervals of fourths and fifths. The *fuguing tune* developed as part of this style of composition. This lively genre featured imitative entries similar to a round. The theme began in one voice and then was picked up by another voice. The song proceeded in this fashion until all the voices had entered with the theme. Many of these early American tunes still appear in our hymnals. However, we often lose the original vigor when we sing them today.

The hymn tune HOLY MANNA is an example from this early American style. To capture the spirit of the frontier singing, experiment with dividing the assembly in half and having the two sides face each other. Proceed to demonstrate the energetic down/up pattern of directing and have each one try it while singing. If everyone puts a lot of energy into the downbeat, the ruggedness of the song will soar. On the second verse, lead the song in a round between the two sides. If that goes well, try dividing each side in half and sing it as a four-part round. Daryl recounts his experience of leading this song at an assembly at the nineteenth-century outdoor tabernacle in historic Mount Gretna, Pennsylvania: "We were transported to a bygone era, and our singing recalled the persistent faith of those early Americans."

IRISH FOLK

While teaching a seminar on enlivening worship, Daryl asked participants if they knew the origin of the song "Be Thou My Vision." No one had a clue that it was an Irish folk tune. "It doesn't sound like one," someone blurted out. Yes, the way it is normally sung does not emulate an Irish folk song. If you play it directly from most hymnals, it will sound more like a traditional Germanic hymn. The harmonies are often intricate, with the chords shifting frequently, sometimes on every beat. The complexity of the song is heightened in some hymnals by extra passing eighth notes and tones that are outside the key. Playing all those notes on the printed page requires taking the song at a slow tempo. When we simplify the harmonies and change

chords primarily only once a measure, the mood changes dras-
tically. Now the tempo can be lively (see page 200). Have a
soloist sing an opening introduction to the song on neutral syllables, like *lie, lie, dee, dee, lie, die.* The singer may model the lilt
of an Irish folk song by giving a light accent and a little scoop in
the voice on beat one. Adding a triangle, tambourine, and hand
drum will enhance the Irish flavor.

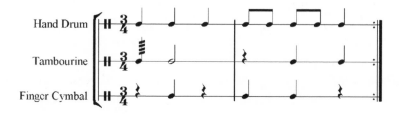

HEBREW TRADITIONAL

For years Daryl recalls singing "The God of Abraham Praise" in
a bold, majestic manner without having given any thought to
the roots of the tune. One day he noticed in *The New Century
Hymnal* the historical note below the hymn: *Yigdal melody.* He
was shocked. With little experience in Hebrew singing, he recalled the tunes from *Fiddler on the Roof.* He remembered the
celebrative wedding scene with energetic dancing, singing, and
clapping. The music was lively, and the rhythms had an under-
lying back beat. This was a far cry from the mood of "The God
of Abraham Praise" as he had heard it sung. He went on a quest
to make the hymn tune sound like a Hebrew melody, rather
than the traditional European sound he was used to.

By simplifying the harmony and changing chords mainly at
the bar line, he was able to speed up the tempo. Then he discovered he could play a type of a vamp on the keyboard with
those simplified harmonies. He played a strong bass note on
each beat in the left hand and followed it with the chord on the

back beat in the right hand. The dancelike nature of the song then became evident. He played around with the rhythms, and soon the Hebrew flavor of the wedding scene emerged with clapping and tambourine.

When he first tried singing it this way with pastors at a clergy convocation, he was dumbfounded by the energy and enthusiasm. The song was totally transformed. (See appendix B, page 201, for a Hebrew setting of "The God of Abraham Praise.")

AFRICAN AMERICAN SPIRITUAL

We had a cursory look at African American spirituals in chapter 3 with the sorrow song "Go Down, Moses." African American spirituals include the stylistic traits of call and response, improvisation, flexible rhythm, covered voice quality, vocal freedom, sense of timelessness, and unaccompanied singing. Try applying some of these principles to the freedom song "I'm So Glad, Jesus Lifted Me." One of the challenges is to present this song in a way that will capture the freedom of the style. Since we cannot assume that everyone present will know the song, we will need to teach it. By teaching it orally, however, we do not have to be bound by the notes on the printed page or hampered by holding a hymnbook. Here is how the two of us recommend teaching it to the assembly.

In keeping with the African American tradition of singing spirituals, join me in singing "I'm So Glad, Jesus Lifted Me." I will sing "I'm so glad" [*point to yourself and sing*], and you sing "Jesus lifted me." [*Sing it first for singers to hear; then point to them and have them sing. Continue to teach the second phrase in the same manner.*] The third time, I sing "I'm so glad," and you respond by singing "Jesus lifted me, singing glory, hallelujah, Jesus lifted me." [*Again, sing it first and then point to them and have them repeat it. Since this is a longer phrase, you may need to practice it several times until they get it.*] Now let's try the whole verse. This time we will add clapping. [*Make sure you lead the assembly in clapping on beats 2 and 4.*]

The song leader may then proceed with singing other verses such as "Satan had me bound," "When I was in trouble," and "When I'm feeling blue." The assembly's response is the same on each verse. Feel free to make up verses and sing as long as the spirit moves you. When the assembly has mastered the clapping, we invite people to start swaying slowly from side to side. Start by leaning on the left foot on beat 1. Clap on beats 2 and 4. In the next measure lean on the right foot on beat 1 and clap on beats 2 and 4. Continue this pattern for the rest of the song.

Taking time to teach this hymn to the assembly will make congregants feel more comfortable singing without a hymnbook. Listen carefully to make sure they are singing it correctly. If they are not getting it, encourage them with words like, "Almost. Listen again. . . . Great, now you have it." By singing the song in this manner, we are able to experience the emotion, freedom, and joy that are so prevalent in jubilation songs.

GOSPEL

The gospel song comes out of the African American tradition and is characterized by a free, improvisatory nature. The style of the piano or organ accompaniment best sets the mood for this type of singing. When learning to play gospel-style piano, Daryl went about it from a theoretical standpoint, not by living in the tradition as most gospel pianists do. He studied piano arrangements such as *Amazing Grace: Blues Gospel Piano* by Jack Schrader.[1] Improvisation was not initially in Daryl's fingers. It first needed to be in his head. While he was tinkering with this style at Lancaster Theological Seminary, many African American students would stop by after chapel and say things like, "You've got to feel the music—just play, and let your fingers guide you," and "You are playing way too fast!" Daryl confesses that by slowing the tempo, he finally was able to start improvising. With the slower tempo he was able to feel an inner triplet, or what he later learned was "swing."

To help readers who have not grown up playing keyboard in this tradition, Daryl has organized a step-by-step process for learning to play in the gospel style. Granted, this approach may seem contrary to the improvisatory nature of gospel playing, but by understanding a few basic principles, a keyboard player will acquire the tools to gain confidence in this style. We will use the spiritual "We Are Climbing Jacob's Ladder" as a model. Keyboard players should start with the first step and practice it until a degree of proficiency is achieved before going to the next step. (See appendix B, page 202.)

1. Play the melody with three notes of the chord in the right hand. Play the bass line in octaves with the left hand.

2. Now add a light swing to the rhythm. Keep the tempo slow, so you can feel the division of the beat as a triplet. Say this rhythm as you play: "1 uh 2 uh 3 uh" (or "1 & uh 2 & uh 3 & uh").

3. Add some repeated chords to the rhythm while saying "1 uh 2 uh . . ." (see measures 1–3).

4. Add extra notes to bass line:
    + Fill in with the fifth of the chord on some of the weak beats (measures 1–3).
    + Add some walking bass notes (measures 4–5).

5. Add extra notes to right hand.
    *   Fill in triplet notes on long-value notes and/or at the end of phrases (measure 8).
    *   Add seconds or sixths to chords (measure 1).
    *   Add blues notes, for example, the flatted third of some chords (measure 14).

GLOBAL

As Michael Hawn notes, just as the "colors of creation . . . form a harmonious rainbow," our life together is perhaps better described as a mosaic of diverse beauty rather than a melting pot of bland similarity. Singing songs of the world church helps us utter more complete praise to our Creator.[2] In chapter 3 we presented a rationale for singing global songs in worship. We recommend using Michael Hawn's book *Halle, Halle: We Sing the World Round* as a starting point for those interested in singing global songs in worship. The teacher's edition gives an overview and examples of African, Latino, and Asian song. Each song presented includes three components that are extremely useful for the small church with limited resources: historical background, liturgical context, and performance practice recommendations.[3] A compact disc is available that demonstrates how to sing the songs in the culture's style and teaches the pronunciations of the languages used.[4]

Most of the songs are simple and easy to learn without the use of music notation. Hawn gives suggestions for using instruments that will help put the songs into their cultural context. Many of the instrumental parts have patterns that are easy for choir members to pick up with relatively little practice. Daryl often hands out instruments to the congregation before the service at St. Peter's. He recommends using simple patterns that can be demonstrated and learned in a few minutes. This is a great way to get more people than just choir members actively involved in the singing. When the accompaniment springs forth from the congregation, it is a reminder to all that the communal song is the work of the people.

African

The African style of singing today is a mixture of two elements: part singing brought in by nineteenth-century missionaries and the indigenous rhythms and tunes from Africa. The music was passed orally from generation to generation. The songs are generally easy to learn and will help your congregation better understand and relate to the life and culture of our brothers and sisters in Africa. Here is a synopsis of stylistic traits of African singing.

- *Steady beat*—The beat remains constant, even at the ends of stanzas and refrains. It usually is a walking tempo in 4/4 time with a slight accent on beat 1.
- *Repetition*—The songs are short and usually sung numerous times. As the song is repeated, the intensity heats up with the gradual addition of voice and instrumental parts. The intent is to reflect the improvisatory nature of African singing. The leader may cue the instrumental players and part singers when they are to begin.
- *Accompaniment*—Usually the songs do not have harmonic support from instruments. Instead, the accompaniment is from percussive instruments like djembe drums, shakers, gourds, claves, gongs, and from clapping or stomping.
- *Rhythm*—The layering of simple rhythmic patterns creates a cacophony of percussion sound. Keep patterns to one to two measures in length. Try creating contrasting rhythms for the various instruments.

+ *Movement*—This is not optional in African singing. Try a simple four-step movement: step forward on beat 1, step back on beat 2, and walk in place on beats 3 and 4. You may also try swaying or stomping.

+ *Voice quality*—The timbre of the voice is a bright, straight tone. Listening to the CD will help you capture the inflections of the Shona, Swahili, and Xhosa languages.

+ *Learned orally*—Most of the songs are short enough to teach by lining out a phrase at a time. It may take several run-throughs to learn a phrase or section properly. If the assembly becomes proficient at learning this way, be venturesome and teach part singing in the same manner. The singing will be enhanced by placing several good singers in each section.

+ *Call and response*—Many of the songs begin with a leader singing several notes or a short phrase before the assembly sings the rest of the song. At the end of the stanza, the leader may call out the words to a new stanza. The leader may also indicate when the song moves back and forth between the native language and English. Sometimes the leader may add to the layering effect by singing a descant.

Latino

The background and influences of Latino music are broad and diverse. Mexico, the Caribbean, Andean countries, Brazil and Argentina, Central America, and Spain each have their own unique stylistic traits. The scope of this study does not allow us to look at each group. We will, however, note some general characteristics of Latino music.

+ *Unison singing*—Unlike African part singing, most Latino songs are in unison.

+ *Song form*—Most Latino songs are in two parts: a stanza followed by a refrain or *estribillo*. The *estribillo* is usually short and easy for the assembly to learn, while the stanzas are often more complex. An inviting way to sing Latino music is to have the assembly sing the eas-ier *estribillo* and a cantor sing the various stanzas. The *estribillo* is often simple enough to be taught orally. In this way the worshiper is freed from the printed page and is able to clap or use rhythm instruments during the singing.

+ *Harmonic accompaniments*—The Latino song is accom-panied by instruments that provide harmonic support. The guitar, accordion, keyboard, xylophone, and man-dolin are commonly used.

+ *Diverse instrumental color*—In addition to the variety of harmonic instruments used, many other instruments enrich the tonal palette of Latino music. They include the rain stick, pan flutes, maracas, claves, congas, bon-gos, timbales, guiros, and tambourine.

+ *Dance rhythms*—The rhythms are often derived from indigenous dance like the *bolero, vals, mazurka, salsa, tango, zamba,* and *cueca*. We recommend that keyboard or guitar players learn some of the basic dance patterns and apply them when accompanying the Latino song. For a listing of basic Latino rhythms see *Leading the Church's Song*.[5]

+ *Polyrhythms/polymeter*—Various instrumental rhythms are layered similarly to African patterns. However, Lati-no rhythms often are made more complex by employing two meters at the same time (usually three beats against two). The Jamaican folk melody of "Let Us Talents and Tongues Employ" exhibits two meters. Measure one is a *guaracha* rhythm (eighth note groupings of 3+3+2) fol-lowed by a duple pattern in measure two (quarter note groupings of 2+2).

These two patterns alternate between measures throughout the stanza. It is easy to use these patterns as the accompaniment for the song. Using simple word patterns makes it easy to feel the polymeter effect without dealing with technical terms. Divide the assembly into three groups or have the choir do group 1 and group 2 and the assembly do group 3.

Group 1: Chant the words "Alleluia, shout for joy" (some play maracas).

Group 2: Chant the words "Jesus lives again" (add conga).

Group 3: Sing the song as written.

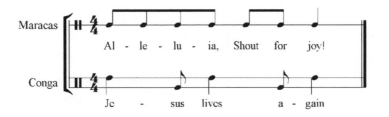

+ *Singing in Spanish*—Singing in Spanish will often enhance the emotion and context of a Latino song. For non-Spanish singers, singing in Spanish may be difficult when several syllables are elided into one note. In Cesareo Gabarain's song "Camina Pueblo de Dios," the *estribillo* is rather easy to sing in Spanish. The stanzas, however, are filled with examples of two syllables squeezed into one note—a task that becomes difficult for non-Spanish-speaking singers.

This song works well if a cantor lines out the *estribillo* one phrase at a time, so the assembly can hear how to sing the words. The cantor may then sing the more complex stanza alone. The refrains may also be sung in English when they are too difficult to sing in Spanish.

Asian

In the past two decades indigenous Asian tunes have started to take root in Asian Christian churches with the work of ethnomusicologists like I-to Loh. Before that time the hymnody of the Asian church consisted primarily of the songs introduced by Western missionaries. With the production of the hymnal *Sound the Bamboo* in 1990, Asian songs took on a soundscape totally different from the Western influence. These ethnic tunes reflect natural speech patterns. They often are free from metric constraints and contain melodies based on non-Western scales. Many times Western notation does not fully represent the nature of the songs. Listening to recordings such as Michael Hawn's *Halle, Halle: We Sing the World Round*[6] and John Bell's and Alison Adam's *Sing with the World: Global Songs for Children*[7] will help church musicians get a feel for the sound of Asian songs.

Churches in North America have much to learn from the Eastern approach to music and worship. The sonorous quality of Eastern music is conducive to prayer, meditation, and stillness. The Western way of expressing reality is time-conscious and goal-oriented. For example, most Western services contain a series of worship events connected in a manner that produces what Western people experience as a logical shape and design. The Eastern way is more concerned with being fully present in the moment. The ancient Eastern practice of meditation encourages an environment in which worshipers can free their minds from clutter, worry, and anxiety and deeply experience the *holy.*

In the Enlivening Worship seminar Daryl led a meditation that reflected some Eastern practices. This meditation may be used at the beginning of a service as a time of transition from the outside world into a sacred space of meeting God. Santee Chapel was dimly lit with candles interspersed throughout the space. The altar was adorned with tea lights and a simple brass cross. Before entering the chapel, worshipers were given instructions and taught the first phrase of an ancient Kyrie, "*Khudaya, rahem kar*" from Pakistan.[8] We sang the song in a quiet, hushed manner reflecting some of the Eastern nuances: vocal slurs between upward leaps, bending of pitches, sustaining tones on the "m," and a slight trill near the end of the phrase. Worshipers entered the chapel prayerfully singing the chant. The chant was sung numerous times before worshipers sat in silence meditating on the image of the cross and listening to their own breathing. The playing of wind chimes signaled to worshipers to begin the chant again. After going through the cycle of silence and singing for about fifteen minutes, a simple "Amen" was said to conclude the time of centering. After the experience we asked the participants for comments. Here are a few of their responses:

"We were transported to another time and place."

"I totally forgot about time and what was going to happen next."

"At first it took me a while to be comfortable with the silence. Finally I was able to relax with it. The worries started to subside."

"I had a deep awareness of God within me."

"I sensed solidarity with my brothers and sisters in other parts of the world."

"The music was free of tension and resolution. It created an atmosphere for meditation."

In singing Eastern songs, care should be taken to not make them sound too Western. Many hymnals still present a Western approach to harmonization. The Eastern scales do not set up a hierarchy of notes as in the Western major and minor scale system. In the Western major scale, for example, the fourth scale step (fa) has a strong pull to go to the third scale step (mi), and the seventh scale step (ti) naturally moves to the eighth scale step (do). In Eastern scales the tones are more nearly equal in importance. "Golden Breaks the Dawn" is based on a Chinese folk tune.[9] Unfortunately, some hymnbooks present the song in the style of a four-part hymn with traditional Western chords. Try singing it in unison, and create an ethereal accompaniment with handbells or glockenspiel. A simple repetitive pattern may be created by taking the notes of the first two measures and placing them in a rising and falling sequence.

Gold - en breaks the   dawn,——

Here are a few general characteristics of Asian song:

+ Music is based on natural speech patterns.
+ Rhythm does not drive the notes.
+ Most songs are sung in unison.
+ Many non-Western scales are used (including ones that divide the octave into intervals of less than a half-step).
+ If harmonization is used for accompaniment, chords are not employed in a Western style. Rather, a unified tonal atmosphere is created by using repetitive patterns

or parallel movement of chords based on open fourths
or fifths.

CONTEMPORARY SONGS

A plethora of modern-day Christian composers are writing in
a wide variety of song styles. The culture in the North American church often puts a box around contemporary songs to
make them fit a single genre. In reality the output is so wide
and varied that we cannot adequately address the subject in
this study. We believe that singing a "new" song to God involves
music other than what has been labeled as "praise and worship"
music. This term actually is offensive to some contemporary
hymn writers whose primary purpose is to lead the assembly in
praise and worship to God through the songs they write, even
though their style may not involve a contemporary praise band.

In fact, it is difficult to define the term *praise music* as it
is traditionally used. In the preface of the new songbook *Sing!
Prayer and Praise,* the United Church of Christ Praise Song
Advisory Team defines *praise music* as "a memorable, melody-
based composition that is musically accessible without being
simplistic; it has a fresh sound incorporating less traditional
rhythms and harmonization."[10] Augsburg Fortress's publica-
tion *Leading the Church's Song* acknowledges the numerous
subgenres of contemporary music:

> Among others, contemporary music embraces folk, country,
> rock 'n' roll, praise, alternative, and the eclectic music of the
> post–Vatican II Roman Catholic tradition. These genres
> share a common emphasis on strong accented rhythm, orally
> conceived melodies, . . . and accompaniment styles based on
> unique technical possibilities and limitations of the guitar.[11]

We recommend that the songs used in worship be easy to
sing and fit the theology and mission of a particular church.
In the Enlivening Worship seminars we studied a sampling of

"Praise and Worship" songs using the four-step filter process by Terri McClean mentioned in chapter 4.[12]

Bruce and Daryl were surprised at how many songs were excluded by the participants as appropriate for their church when they went through the filter process. Most said that before their exposure to this process, their song evaluation centered mainly on whether they liked or didn't like a song. The filter process proved to be a valuable tool to help wade through the countless number of "Praise and Worship" songs on the market. Here is an overview of McClean's process for song selection:

1. Assessing theology. (Do the words correspond to our theological beliefs?)
2. Matching music to mission. (Does the text support our mission statement?)
3. Evaluating the songwriting. (How does the music draw people into worship? Is it accessible and easy to sing?)
4. Plugging the music into worship. (How and when is the song best used in worship?)[13]

When the worship team finds a song that stands the test of these filters, team members may proceed with confidence, knowing that the song will work well in their church. The next step is to develop a strategy for presenting the song so that the assembly may fully participate, while at the same time adding some contemporary musical components to the songs. Small churches often think they cannot adequately use contemporary songs because they do not have the resources for an elaborate praise band. Contemporary singing can be led in many ways: leadership can be provided simply by a keyboard with a song leader, or it may involve a much larger praise band with guitars, percussion, keyboards, and vocalists. Here is a wonderful opportunity to discover and employ the various musical gifts of the church. Unknown gifts may emerge as this process is begun.

As musicians with various gifts are discovered, it is time to build an ensemble. Keep in mind that contemporary music is a popular style. The most basic element must be an instrument that provides harmonic support. Keyboard and guitar, played independently or together, work well to perform this function. Often these instrumentalists play from a lead sheet, which consists of just the melody, text, and chord symbols. Sometimes these players simply play chords to the song while supplying interesting rhythmic support. A variety of rhythms may be achieved on the guitar with creative downward and upward strumming patterns. Keyboard players may employ this style by using oscillating chord patterns in the right hand while providing the foundation of the chord in the left hand. Here is a simple accompaniment to the contemporary song "Amazing Love" by Graham Kendrick.[14]

After creating a foundational harmonic support with a guitar or keyboard, the praise band may be enhanced by layering other sounds. Keep in mind that these other sounds are optional but will enrich the contemporary texture. Percussion instruments are an excellent way to provide rhythmic stability while adding to the tonal palette. A single player may play a trap set, which consists of a kick drum or bass drum, snare drum, toms, and cymbals. Other percussion instruments like congas, bongos, claves, tambourines, and shakers may be easily added to the ensemble. These may be used with or without the trap set.

More rhythmic support may be added by a person playing the bass part on a guitar or second keyboard. This part usually gives a strong emphasis to beat 1 and rhythmic variety on the weaker beats. Adding a bass part enables the assembly to better feel the beat and stay together. Here is a sample of what the bass player could play for the song "Amazing Love."

The final and most important aspect in inviting the assembly to participate in the singing of contemporary music is to reinforce the melody firmly with a lead singer or group of singers. The melody may be further emphasized by a lead guitar or a synthesized sound from a keyboard. Care should be taken that the congregation's singing is supported by the lead singers and not overpowered by any member of the band. Rock bands by their very nature produce a loud sound because of the drums and amplification. When a band plays as if worship were a rock concert, the voice of the people singing is suppressed by the sheer volume. Each band member and sound technician must understand that his or her primary purpose is to lead the assembly to participate in the worship experience. This may be a challenging countercultural concept for worship leaders to keep reinforcing as they relate to parishioners who play or experience rock music outside the church.

At this point the worship team must wrestle with how a contemporary song will be conveyed to the assembly. Will the words be projected on an overhead screen in hopes that the congregation will eventually catch on and join in? Is the music printed on a sheet that worshipers must hold, perhaps inhibiting clapping? Is it beneficial to take time to teach the assembly the song during the announcement portion of the service? There are no easy answers to these questions. Each song and situation will demand a different solution. To think there is only one way to "do" contemporary singing is a grave error.

A small church may find *contemporary songs* a meaningful addition to other song styles after working through these theological and technical aspects of the genre. The popular and familiar sound may be a source of welcome to visitors or to those who do not have a history within the Christian church. Those folks may feel at home with a less structured approach to liturgy, an informal style of dress, and the contemporary language of the songs. Explore using this genre in conjunction with other song styles. Do not fall into the trap of assuming that this style can be done only in what has been commonly referred to as "contemporary worship."

A congregation that uses diverse styles of singing has great potential to connect its own worship and music with the worship of Christians throughout the world. Using an eclectic repertoire may help the church find its mission expanding beyond measure. Pray that singing the songs from other times and places will open hearts to see new insights into God's vast realm.

ENLIVENING MUSIC
AND WORSHIP IN YOUR CHURCH

Have your worship team take an inventory of the songs styles you used in worship over the past year. Use a chart or a spreadsheet with these and other styles as headings: chant, Renaissance/Baroque dance, European classical, Western European folk, Hebrew, African, Latino, Asian, Native American, early American, African American spiritual, gospel, and contemporary. Put each song you used under one of these headings, or under other headings you devise. Begin a dialogue about your church's song style by answering these questions:

1. What style is most prevalent?
2. What styles do you use on a fairly regular basis (four or more times throughout the year)?
3. What styles have you tried minimally (one to three times)?
4. What styles would you like to add to your repertoire?

As your team explores the styles of songs you used over the past year, think about how your church has sung each style. What techniques in this chapter can be used to enhance the singing? Assess the talents within your congregation. Are there new areas of worship you would like to explore? You may want to explore other genres by using the techniques in this chapter. Study the context in which the song was written, determine the basic stylistic traits, and establish how to bring the song to life. Finally, develop a plan for the coming year to enliven the styles you already use and to expand your repertoire.

CHAPTER 6

THE PASTOR AND THE CHURCH MUSICIAN

FRIEND, FOE, OR FIASCO

THE APOSTLE PAUL once described the church as the body of Christ, a dynamic, creative, and interdependent reality in which our spiritual lives find support and nurture (1 Cor. 12:12–30). Long before contemporary physics and the current ecological movement, Paul recognized that the quality of our lives, in good measure, arises from the quality of our relationships, both individually and in our faith communities. Paul notes, "If one member suffers, all suffer together with it; if one member is honored, all rejoice together with it" (1 Cor. 12:26).

Face-to-face relationships characterize life in a small congregation, where truly "there is no place to run, and no place to hide" for pastors, church musicians, or congregants. Over the years, the two of us have observed the lively and creative synergy that occurs when pastors and church musicians work together in light of a common vision. Sadly, we have also observed the negative impact of poor communication and the lack of a common vision among church musicians and pastors. Like Euodia and Syntyche, to whom the apostle Paul writes words of challenge and reconciliation in the Letter to the Philippians (Phil. 4:2–3), alienation between a pastor and church musician can lead to disharmony and polarization in the life of a small congregation.

In this chapter, we explore ways in which pastors and church musicians can find spiritual and vocational common ground, despite the differences that may exist in education, vocation, personality type, liturgical focus, and spiritual gifts. The two of us believe that creative and affirmative partnerships among pastors and church musicians are essential for vital worship and music in the small church.

PASTOR AND CHURCH MUSICIAN AS FRIENDS

Daryl has been a church musician for thirty years. Over the years he has participated in various and sundry types of relationships with his partners in crime—or in ministry—namely, pastors. At times, he has experienced a relationship that was warm and congenial. You might even call it a "friendly relationship."

Bruce has also appreciated the lively synergy of planning worship with theologically astute and liturgically creative church musicians in his thirty years of pastoral ministry and programmatic leadership.

In the course of their roles as church musician and pastor, Daryl and Bruce have recognized some common characteristics of healthy and creative partnerships among pastors and church musicians. Broadly speaking, professional friendships among pastors and church musicians involve the following values and behaviors:

1. Shared common goals in ministry and worship: when pastors and church musicians work together in tandem toward a vital worship ministry, congregational worship comes alive as new and creative harmonies emerge.

2. Positive communication, similar to that described by the apostle Paul in Philippians 4:8: "Whatever is true, whatever is honorable, whatever is just, whatever is pure, . . . whatever is commendable . . . think about these things."

3. Understanding each other's strengths and weaknesses in worship leadership, theological expertise, and musical training and perspective. A good example of this creative partnership occurred in Bruce's work with a university choir director during his tenure as Protestant chaplain at Georgetown University. Because Bruce does not read music, he often hummed hymns or had the choir director play melodies, especially when he was trying to join the theology of his sermon with music that could easily be learned by the congregation. Conversely, the university choir director depended on Bruce's theological insight in her choice of choral anthems.

4. Respect for each other's role in ministry and recognition of each other's unique gifts for ministry. In the spirit of Paul's description of the body of Christ, pastor and church musician support each other and honor each other's vocations in ministry. They recognize that they cannot fulfill their vocations in ministry without each other's gifts.

5. Nurturing each other's ministry in word and deed and supporting one another as fellow Christians, both privately and publicly.

PASTOR AND CHURCH MUSICIAN AS FOES

Unfortunately, Daryl has been involved in a pastor-musician relationship that was not as ideal as the one previously described. This relationship was characterized by manipulation, distrust, misunderstanding, poor communication, and a lack of comprehension of each other's duties. In fact, he and the pastor had a downright dislike for each other. You might say that the relationship was one of enmity rather than friendship, despite their claim to be fellow Christians. Unbelievable, you might say. After all, as one participant in a worship seminar noted, "I thought all church workers got along. I thought they all worked together in peace, love, and harmony." Sadly, disharmony and misunderstanding can characterize the relationships of those called to be the congregation's spiritual and worship leaders. This disharmony may eventually poison the worship life of a small congregation.

PASTOR AND THE CHURCH MUSICIAN: THE FIASCO

Sometimes pastors and church musicians, motivated by the best of intentions, can create situations that undermine creative and vital worship as well as healthy collegial relationships. The following dialogue, involving Pastor Fred and Daryl, sadly reflects countless chaotic conversations that have taken place between pastors and church musicians.[1]

Sitting at his desk, Pastor Fred apologizes to the church secretary as he picks up the phone to speak with Daryl, and we hear Pastor Fred's side of the dialogue:

> Excuse me while I take this phone call. Hello—Pastor Fred here. Hey, Daryl, how is it going? What's up? [pause] Oh, yeah, that's right, you need the hymns for tomorrow's service. I kind of got tied up today. I was doing ministry on the golf course. Yep—great day for golf. Beautiful weather ... my putting was really coming together. Oh, yeah, yeah, the hymns. Sorry I couldn't get to you sooner. Well, you're such a good organist; you don't need to practice anyway, do you? [pause] OK. Hang on. Let me get my hymnal. . . . It's here somewhere. Oh, here it is. Hey, let's start off with something really lively. Something really upbeat. You know—grab their attention, wake 'em up for worship! Let's see. Oh, here's one. Lots of notes on the page. That means it goes really fast, doesn't it? Oh, heck. I don't know what the tune sounds like. Why don't you sing it to me? It's on page 339 in the hymnal—"Truth Whom We Adore." [pause] Hey, Daryl, wait a minute . . .

that's not going to work. It sounds too boring. Hey, I have a better idea. Maybe we should start with a golden oldie. . . like "Amazing Grace." *[pause]* Oh, you don't think it's too lively. . . . Well, just play it faster. You can do that. YOU'RE THE MAN! Now, how about the hymn of the day? You know what I mean, the hymn after the sermon. What do you think? Oh, my sermon title . . . uh . . . well . . . I plan to write that tonight. I have been thinking about it all week. *[pause]* The Scripture lessons? Oh, I have them here somewhere. . . . Hey, listen, I'm in kind of a hurry. Why don't you just pick a hymn you like to play. . . . Yeah, you can do it. I trust your judgment. Remember, Daryl—YOU'RE THE MAN! See ya in worship tomorrow.

As you reflect on this encounter, what do you notice? What's wrong with this interchange? What qualities do you notice in the pastor's approach to the hymns and the role of the church musician?

In reflecting on this encounter, Daryl and Bruce noticed the following characteristics (in this case, mostly unintentional) of the otherwise jovial and supportive pastor: lack of respect, poor communication, last-minute planning, lack of understanding of the duties of the musician, a superficial understanding of worship.

"At times, Pastor Fred drove me nuts," Daryl admits. Reflecting on their experience as colleagues, Daryl recalls:

But you know what?—I liked Pastor Fred. He was a "good ol' boy" and was, for the most part, easy to work with. I enjoyed coming into the church office Monday mornings. We typically had a good chat about his weekend golf game, and I talked about my bike rides on the trails. We got along just fine from Monday to Friday. But come Sunday morning, chaos reigned and often ruined my worship experience and, I suspect, the experiences of others in the congregation.

Daryl continues his narrative of a typical Sunday morning service from his standpoint as a church musician:

> At this church, we had announcements first and then the prelude. As a church musician, I like that. After we get the introductions and housekeeping out of the way, we can concentrate on the worship of God. But one Sunday—and this happened repeatedly over the years—I recall just finishing a lively setting of "Marching to Zion" by John Ferguson. I put my music away and was bowing my head in preparation for the Order of Confession and Forgiveness. As a faithful Christian, only too aware of my imperfections, I really need that part of the service. But this morning, I was startled out of my silent contemplation. "Hey, Daryl. What was that you just played . . . a Methodist hymn?" I looked dumbfounded as I felt some two hundred eyes look my way. "Uh . . . I'm not sure," I said. I quickly turned to the piece of music I had just played. I saw the title of the collection and blurted out, "It's a revival hymn!" "Oh, OK," said Pastor Fred. "I was just wondering. . . . I thought it sounded Methodist. . . . Let us now confess our sins, using the brief Order of Confession and Forgiveness found in your bulletin." By that time, I was fuming. If ever I needed to make a confession, it was then. What a fiasco! So much for my attempt to contribute to vital worship or to experience worship at all that day!

From a pastor's standpoint, the fiasco can come also from the side of the church musician. Judy, the pastor of a small, moderately liberal inner-city congregation, struggled for nearly a year with the choices the choir director/organist made. While Judy chose hymns that reflected the theme of her sermon, Pam, the church musician, whose theological orientation was more conservative than Judy's, regularly chose anthems that reflected a theology opposite from the sermon of the day. Judy remembers two such occasions:

On Earth Sunday, I celebrated the beauty of the earth and our responsibility to care for creation. I preached about our calling to love God in *this* life and *this* world. I chose hymns that described God's love for the whole earth. But, oh, that anthem! How could she have chosen a chorale version of "Just as I Am"! Another Sunday, when I preached about the importance of religious tolerance, the postlude was a variation on "Onward, Christian Soldiers, Marching as to War."

Eventually, Judy had to relieve Pam of her duties when, after several conversations, it became clear that she did not respect Judy's theological position or support her need to have consistency between the sermon, anthem, prelude, and postlude.

As you can see, the relationship between pastor and church musician can take on many forms. Perhaps you have also experienced those fiasco moments—those moments that distract you and your congregation from participating in vital and life-transforming worship. The two of us have found that when people experience too many of these fiasco moments, their relationship with their counterparts in worship leadership may turn sour, and before they know it, they may have moved from *friend* to *foe*.

Self-awareness and awareness of the other are essential to every good relationship, whether collegial or marital. The two of us believe that church musicians and pastors need to take an honest look at their respective theological perspectives, approaches to worship, and gifts in worship leadership by asking the following questions: How do we complement one another in worship leadership? What areas are strong, and what areas need a bit of tweaking in our individual and collegial worship leadership? How do we each understand the aim of worship and the role of music in worship? If we come from different theological or liturgical perspectives, in what areas can we find common ground?

This has been an important topic in Daryl's ministry as a church musician. He has experienced the good with the bad.

As Daryl talks to his church-musician colleagues and pastor friends, he finds that this is an important issue for them, too. This is one reason that Daryl teaches a class at Lancaster Theological Seminary titled "The Pastor and the Church Musician: Friends, Foes, or Fiasco." As part of this course, he invites both pastors and church musicians to be part of a panel to discuss this important partnership. The experiences the class hears from worship leaders working in the trenches are enlightening for seminarians looking toward a lifetime of pastoral leadership.

We are sure your stories could add to a lively conversation as well. The two of us have learned much about the joys and challenges of shared worship leadership through our conversations with pastors and church musicians. We have learned about great working relationships, but we have also heard stories that would be hilarious—if they weren't so tragic and polarizing in the life of the church and to its pastoral and liturgical leaders. And do you know what? We still have a lot to learn.

We invite you to take a few minutes to consider your own experiences working with pastors or church musicians. What has been the most rewarding aspect of working with your colleague in worship? What has been the most difficult situation you have faced in sharing worship leadership with your colleague? What traits do you value most in a partner in ministry? How do you describe your current professional situation? In what ways might you improve the quality of your current relationship with your counterpart in worship leadership?

FORMING CREATIVE PARTNERSHIPS IN WORSHIP LEADERSHIP

One thing the two of us have discovered in listening to pastors and church musicians is that there seems to be a direct correlation between the worship life of a community and the relationship between the pastor and the church musician. When this partnership suffers, congregational worship suffers. When the partnership is flourishing, the way is clear for us to foster dynamic worship. To promote vital worship in our church, it is imperative that we have a strong partnership between the pastor and the church musician. Notice we *did* call it a partnership. Partnerships in worship planning and leadership, like all good relationships, are not accidental, but are the result of prayerful intention and a commitment to work together in creating a healthy professional relationship. Over the years, the two of us have discovered four steps to help us achieve creative partnerships in worship leadership.

Good Communication

Healthy and direct communication is at the very heart of a good relationship. The two of us know that pastors and church musicians are all extremely busy carrying out their roles in ministry. It is easy for communication to take a back seat or for one person just to do it alone without consulting colleagues in worship leadership. Making time for regular worship planning sessions is the first step to creative partnership in worship leadership. If you are blessed to have a pastor and a church musician with flexible hours, it is fairly easy to plan meetings during the day when both are in the office. But church musicians in small congregations are either volunteers or part-time employees, and even the pastor might be part-time, so both members of the team will need to be more creative in setting aside times to meet. These sessions may involve more than just the pastor and church musician, although it is good to have set times to meet alone to share your visions and dreams as well your frustrations, hurts, and misunderstandings. As we said earlier, small can be beautiful, but it can also be challenging for pastor and church musician alike.

Whatever the size of a congregation, the pastor and the church musician must work together, seeking above all to find common ground in worship planning and leadership. As

Genesis notes, it is not good to be alone, either in our life journeys or in planning worship in small congregations. It is easy to succumb to hopelessness or to try to carry the burden of creative music and worship all by ourselves. Good communication is tough, and it takes time, but good communication is essential for vital and creative worship over the long haul.

Understanding Strengths, Weaknesses, and Personality Types

The second step in nurturing a positive relationship with the pastor and church musician involves understanding each other's strengths, weaknesses, and personality types. Each of us has many gifts for leadership in the body of Christ. But each of us also depends on the gifts of others to fulfill our vocation and flourish in congregational leadership. For Daryl, it was important to know and accept the fact that Pastor Fred was not a musician and had only a modest knowledge of hymns. Daryl needed to be patient with him when he tried to sing a song he didn't know. Daryl also came to realize that organization was not one of Pastor Fred's strong points. This awareness helped him understand why Pastor Fred had trouble finding memos that had been given to him only a week before. He would joke with Daryl, "I know it's in here somewhere," as he looked through the mounds of papers on his desk. Daryl soon learned that it helped him to make an extra copy of the memo, in case Pastor Fred lost it. This practice decreased Daryl's stress, while enabling the meetings to be productive.

While we don't have Pastor Fred's side of the story, Daryl recognizes that he too needed to make some changes to work more creatively with Pastor Fred. Daryl recognized that he needed to see Pastor Fred as a whole person whose gifts went far beyond worship. "This helped me to remember that Pastor Fred was a 'people person.' That's why people loved him." To him, people were more important than that piece of paper

Daryl gave him the week before. Daryl realized that he could not change Pastor Fred, but he could appreciate the man's personal and professional gifts. Daryl also discovered the importance of patience in professional relationships and spiritual growth as a result of his commitment to work creatively with Pastor Fred.

Personality type is not a matter of strength or weakness, but a description of our personal preferences, including how we gather data, make decisions, and approach the complexities of life. Awareness of one another's unique personality types is essential to any healthy relationship. Daryl notes that it was helpful for him to understand Fred's Myers-Briggs personality type, which was ESFP (Extraversion, Sensing, Feeling, Perceiving). Pastor Fred was inclined to live in the moment rather than to plan weeks in advance and also to prefer personal relationships as sources of information over what he considered impersonal administrative memos.

Daryl recognized that to foster a more healthy working relationship, he needed to talk about his personality type and professional approach with Pastor Fred.

> I wanted him to understand that I needed moments of quiet before worship. I didn't like things thrown at me at the last minute. I also didn't like him to make promises to other people for me. I remember when he promised a couple that I would play a certain song at their wedding. He made the mistake of not checking with me first. He soon learned not to do that. It was important that he knew that my Myers-Briggs personality type was ISFP (Introversion, Sensing, Feeling, Perceiving).

While in many ways Daryl and the extroverted Pastor Fred were quite similar in personality type (SFP), the more introverted Daryl required more contemplative time and greater advance notice than his more relationally active and spontaneous colleague. Eventually, Daryl and Pastor Fred came to understand and appreciate their different ways of encountering the world and making decisions, and adapted their behaviors to "meet in the middle." Their differences became a source of creativity rather than antagonism.[2]

The two of us recognize that it takes work to be a team player. A good partner complements the strengths of the other. A team player gives encouragement and fills in some of the gaps where the other is weak. Together they learn to be flexible. There is a general sense of give-and-take to the relationship. We look beyond our ego and our need for things to be "just so," that God's spirit might move creatively in our worship planning.

Respecting Each Other's Roles in Ministry

While we need to understand and respond positively to each other's strengths and weaknesses, we also need to respect each other's role in ministry. Daryl sees his primary role as a church musician as leading the people in song. Daryl needs his counterpart to trust his ability to bring forth the best singing from the congregation. He or she must trust that Daryl's way of interpreting a specific hymn has been thought out with utmost care and that he has given much attention to registration, tempo, harmonization, rhythm, style, and so forth. All these decisions are based on helping the people understand the nuances of the text and enabling them to sing with integrity.

The converse is also true. Bruce notes that the church musician needs to have an appreciation of the role of the pastor as the primary, though not the only, theologian and spiritual leader of the congregation. Accordingly, the church musician needs to take the pastor's theological insights seriously and to weave them into his or her worship leadership by choosing anthems and hymns that complement the theme of the sermon. The pastor's role is multifaceted, requiring attention to pastoral care issues, preaching/teaching, spiritual formation, prophetic hospitality, and administration.[3] The pastor needs the church musician to understand that emergencies come up. In addition, confidentiality is essential to healthy pastoral ministry, and the pastor may not always be able to explain to the church musician what is really going on in the life of a congregant. In planning worship, the pastor may be looking at a much broader picture, which includes other things than just the music.

To understand each other's roles more fully, it is important to know as much about your partner's job as possible. Start out by reading each other's job descriptions—if they exist in your congregation. Perhaps you could share professional articles with each other. Ask your colleague to go to a workshop with you, such as a meeting of the local chapter of the American Guild of Organists (AGO) or a lecture or program at the local seminary. It takes work to get outside our own professional worldviews and to embrace the professional context of the other. The dividends, however, are well worth the effort.

If both pastor and church musician focus on growing together, each can learn something important about the other's discipline. Bruce has found it helpful to learn stories and the historical or social settings from which certain hymns and songs have emerged. Daryl has been fortunate to grow in theological insight as a result of sharing in his wife Bonnie's ministry and through teaching at a seminary.

Creating a Spiritually Nourishing Environment

A final area in creating a team ministry is generating an environment that nurtures each other's spirituality. This is one of the most important things you can do, but it is often neglected amid the busyness of our ministerial tasks. Understanding the importance of spiritual practices for both pastor and church musician is essential for vital and effective ministry.[4]

Prayer is at the heart of our relationship with God, both in worship and in our private lives. We need solitude to hear God's voice in our lives and in our public responsibilities. Regular times of prayer and meditation nurture our spiritual lives and connect our creative spirit with God's creative spirit moving in our lives.

How often do we look at the pastor as the *only* one who provides spiritual nurture or theological insight in the congregation? How often do we neglect the role of the church musician as the pastor's partner in promoting theological reflection and spiritual formation in congregational life? (We will address the significance of theological reflection and leadership in the work of church musicians in chapter 8.) How often is the pastor so busy caring for the souls of others that she neglects taking care of herself?

The two of us believe that both the pastor and the church musician must be committed to personal and congregational spiritual formation. Holistic spirituality involves both individuals and communities. Jesus often spent time in prayer, but he also invited his disciples to go on spiritual retreats as a group. In this spirit, pastors and church musicians can mutually support each other's spiritual lives.

Congregations need to be educated on the importance of prayer and study for both pastors and church musicians. Daryl notes that he was once employed by a church whose leaders thought the spiritual formation of church musicians so important that they gave him one day a month for spiritual retreat and renewal. He used this time in a variety of ways—for a silent retreat at a Jesuit center, a prayer retreat at a cabin, and time set aside for readings in spirituality. Whatever the form, it was time away from the office devoted solely to prayer, meditation, silence, and listening for God's presence in his life.

Another important aspect of spiritual nourishment is a daily commitment to prayer and meditation. Daryl worked with a pastor who believed in this habit so much that a "Please do not disturb" sign was placed on her office door at the beginning of each day. The staff and congregants knew that this was her prayer time and a model for the whole staff and congregation. You may choose an even more subtle or private approach to your spiritual formation. While Bruce has seldom received such explicit congregational or institutional support for his spiritual life, he has made it a practice to spend the first two hours of each day in contemplation, prayer walking (aerobic in style), and study and writing. This daily practice has deepened his preaching, spiritual leadership, teaching, pastoral care, and leadership of clergy groups and has been instrumental in the writing of nearly twenty books.

Many congregations have prayer or meditation rooms. For Daryl, the altar in the nave is a wonderful place for prayer. Daryl notes, "What better place to pray than at the altar where we corporately worship and receive God's nourishment? How blessed is my practice time when I begin it with silence at the altar!" Prayer and meditation may be done anywhere, however—on a walk or in a special place at home; in the morning or at other times of the day. It is clear to us that finding your quiet corner and making it a spiritual discipline is important to ministry.

How would your ministry change if the pastor and church musician went to spiritual retreats together? How would it be enhanced if you made a commitment for a time of morning or evening prayer with the church staff? Spiritual practices help to deepen and replenish our lives so that we have something to give in our times of worship leadership. God cannot fully use our gifts when we are so busy that we have no time to hear God's voice in our daily lives. Our leadership in worship is richer when we have practiced prayer and meditation throughout the week.

In the partnership of pastor and church musician, attention to spiritual practices may need to be nurtured and encouraged by your colleague in ministry. If you feel you need to take more time for spiritual practices as a church musician, you may need to voice that to the pastor. As a pastor, you may need to encourage this aspect for the church musician and for your congregation as a whole. Pastors, of course, need to practice what they preach and take time for deepening their own spiritual lives. We hope that together you will find ways of encouraging each other in this important spiritual development.

Creative worship calls us to be bold in creating healthy relationships between the pastor and church musician that are loving, supportive, full of open communication, and grounded in spirituality. With God's help, may we all be part of a dynamic team that can be influential in leading our congregations to vital and faithful worship.

ENLIVENING WORSHIP AND MUSIC IN YOUR CHURCH

Partnership in leading the church's worship is deepened by a commitment to practicing the presence of God. Our first exercise involves the spiritual practice of focusing on our breath. Breath is essential to worship as well as to spiritual growth. Jesus breathed on his disciples and said, "Receive the Holy Spirit." The Psalms end with the affirmation "let everything that breathes praise [God]" (Ps. 150:6).

In this exercise, find a comfortable position to sit with your back straight and your feet planted flat on the floor. Close your eyes and take a moment to ask for God's inspiration in your life. Then gently inhale, noticing your breath. With each inhalation, experience God's presence filling your whole being, body, mind, and spirit. As you exhale, let go of any anxiety or pressure. With each breath, rest in God's sustaining, empowering, inspiring, and calming care. In the spirit of the hymn "Breathe on Me, Breath of God," open yourself to God's new and abundant life with each breath. As you exhale, you may choose to sing this chant as part of your meditation.

Daryl Hollinger

Breathe   on   me,   Breath   of   God.

Take at least five minutes twice a day for this time of peaceful centering. Breath prayers such as this can be incorporated into choir practice as well as personal spiritual formation. Choir practice is, after all, intended to be worshipful and spiritually edifying as well as designed to prepare the choir technically for Sunday morning. After a Scripture reading, you can invite the choir members to breathe gently, feeling their connection with God and one another.

Our second exercise involves using our imagination to see the gifts of our partners in worship leadership. We invite you to take a moment to center yourself with the breath prayer described above. Then, take a moment to read 1 Corinthians 12:12–30 prayerfully in the spirit of "holy reading" or *lectio divina*, listening for what the words mean for your role as a pastor, church musician, or choir member.

As you experience a sense of peace or centeredness, reflect on your gifts within the body of Christ. What gifts do you have as a pastor, church musician, or choir member? Visualize how you contribute to your faith community through your giftedness. Thank God for the opportunity to share your gifts within the body of Christ.

Now, take some time to reflect on the gifts of your colleagues in worship leadership, whether the pastor, the church musician, or a choir member. What gifts do your colleagues contribute to the body of Christ? Visualize their contribution to your faith community through their gifts. Thank God for their unique gifts to the community and its worship.

The two of us have discovered that when we take time to notice, appreciate, and give thanks for the gifts of others, we respond more creatively to their gifts, idiosyncrasies, and behavioral challenges. We can deal more creatively with interpersonal conflicts and differences in personality type when we are able to experience the presence of God in those with whom we plan and lead worship.

CHAPTER 7

WORSHIP PLANNING

DESIGN, SHAPE, AND FLOW

AFTER THREE MONTHS of working with small churches in the Enlivening Worship seminar, we discovered the creative potential of small congregations to transform their worship services. Seminar participants were not only looking at ways to enrich their worship through meaningful and diverse music; they were also thinking about innovative approaches for using visual arts, drama, dance, poetry, and creative reading. We were encouraged by their enthusiasm. We were delighted that they had found methods to engage their congregations in vital and faithful worship.

As teams brought their many ideas to the planning table, they soon realized that it was difficult to craft creative ideas into a cohesive and meaningful service. As we approached the challenge of worship planning these questions emerged:

- How do we discern the overall design of the service?
- How do we plan worship to support the overall theme of the day?
- How do we connect ideas so that the service has a logical flow?
- How do we use various moods within a service to achieve a balance between tradition and novelty?

+   How do we keep our egos in check as we suggest ideas
    to the group?

In this chapter we offer tools to help teams find answers to
these questions. As the seminar groups worked through these
concepts for worship planning, the pastors, musicians, visual
artists, actors, and dancers began to understand how their part
in a worship service related to the broader picture of the whole.
Individual components of the liturgy were not thought of as
separate entities but as parts of a unified and cohesive service.

We will look at three important aspects of a worship service: design, shape, and flow. Daryl relates these concepts to his
photograph below of Great Smoky Mountain National Park.
The overall design has three components: the trees in the foreground, the mountains in the middle, and the cloudy sky in
the background. Each component has a shape. For example,
the shape of the foreground follows the outline of the treetops.
The gradual incline of the hills from left to right is interrupted
by a tall evergreen tree and then by several dead trees on the
right. The flow of the picture may be thought of as the way the

separate elements are connected. Note, for example, the fairly sharp contrast between the trees in the foreground and the mountains of the middle ground. On the other hand, the flow between the middle ground and the sky in the background is less well defined. As your eye moves to the right, the delineation between mountains and sky is almost imperceptible.

A worship service may be described similarly. The *design* of a service is the overall scheme, usually including two to five major sections. The *shape* of the service components relates to their mood and energy level, and the *flow* is the way the parts are connected. In the Enlivening Worship seminar, we used a short worship service, based on a brief service at St. Peter's that was part of our Advent Family Festival, to show how shape and flow work together in the design of the service. This service can easily be adapted for other contexts, such as an extended call to worship for the first Sunday in Advent or a Sunday school forum about celebrating the season of Advent.

WAITING FOR THE LIGHT: AN ADVENT SERVICE

Breathing

Leader: We wait in silence. As you inhale, invite God's presence to be with you. As you exhale, imagine tension and anxiety leaving your body. (*Allow several minutes of silence. Daryl played his Native American flute to accent this time of waiting.*)

Song: "Wait for the Lord"[1] (*Sing prayerfully several times.*)

Drama: "Get Out of My Way" (see appendix A, page 195).

Song: "Wait for the Lord"

Drama: "I Just Gotta Have It Now!" (see appendix A, page 196).

Song: "Wait for the Lord"

Drama: "Christmas Carol Crisis" (see appendix A, page 197).

Song: "Wait for the Lord"

Invitation to Confession

Leader: Sometimes instead of waiting for God's direction, we expend our energy fretting about how busy we are. We miss opportunities for joy, for growth, for wisdom, for blessing— simply because we do not listen to what God has in store for us. We doubt that God has something wonderful waiting for us. We scurry around trying to make our own joy. Let us pause for a moment of silence as we wait for God.

Silence

Assurance of God's Grace

Leader: Friends, we do not need to be worried or be discouraged in these times. God steps into the midst of our busy lives and plants opportunities for joy and light. You are invited to come and light a candle as a symbol of the light of the coming Christ. Let the light of Christ come into the nooks and crannies of your life and bring you calm. Come, receive the light.

Song and Lighting of Candles (see appendix B, page 203, for song accompaniment).

Out of the shad-ows of fear;___ and in-to the light we come. ___

God gives us hope for the jour - ney. God brings us peace to - day.

Prayer

All: O God of Light, Emmanuel, God with us, we ask you to send your light into our hearts. Help us to be ready for the day and the hour of Christ's appearing. Live in us and help us to live in you. By the power of the Holy Spirit, touch us.

Transform us so that our worship, our celebration, our time of preparation, may be pleasing unto you—both now and forevermore. Amen.

Song: "Wait for the Lord"
Silence
Leader: Amen.

DESIGN IN WORSHIP

The design of this service includes two major sections:

1. Listening
2. Responding

The first part involves waiting and listening for God to speak through the meditative and repetitive song "Wait for the Lord" and the contemporary scenes of the dramas. The second part provides an opportunity to respond to God through confession. By lighting candles and singing "Out of the Shadows of Fear," worshipers affirm the presence of the incarnate Christ in their lives.

A Service of Word and Table usually follows a fourfold pattern:

1. Gathering
2. Word
3. Meal
4. Sending

The late Robert Webber, author of more than forty books on worship and liturgy, explores how this design was used in the Christian church for centuries.[2] He shows ways this pattern is used creatively today in liturgical traditions as well as in free-style worship services. *Evangelical Lutheran Worship*, a worship resource for Evangelical Lutheran Church in America

(ELCA) congregations, also notes the importance of this design. The basic pattern of this service—gathering, word, meal, sending—allows congregations freedom and flexibility in shaping worship while maintaining what the church holds in common.[3]

The *Gathering* section may include a wide array of worship events, depending on the denomination or style of worship. In liturgical churches the parts of the gathering may include a prelude, confession, greeting, gathering songs (hymns, psalms, Kyrie, Gloria or canticle of praise), and a prayer or invocation. A free-style worship service may include a prelude, call to worship, numerous gathering songs, sharing time, and prayer.

In the second part of the fourfold design, God speaks to us through the *Word*.

Listening to Scripture readings and preaching is the norm. Many churches read texts prescribed by the Revised Common Lectionary. Churches that follow a formal liturgy often include four readings: Hebrew Scripture, Psalm (read or sung), Epistle, and Gospel. Psalm refrains, proper verses, and Gospel acclamations may be sung. Free-style services may include Scripture lessons based on themes or topics. In most services, preaching, based on one or more of the Scripture passages, follows the readings. A time of response usually comes after the sermon and may include singing, creeds, and intercessory prayers.

The *Meal* is the third section of this design. Many services begin with the offering to support the mission and ministry of the local and broader church. As these gifts are brought forward, the table is often prepared with the bread and wine. The meal may include the following: Offertory prayer, the Great Thanksgiving (Dialogue, Preface, "Holy, Holy, Holy" [*Sanctus*], Words of Institution, Lord's Prayer), Breaking of the Bread and Pouring of the Wine, "Lamb of God" (*Agnus Dei*), Call to the Meal, Sharing of the Elements, and Prayer of Thanksgiving.

In the *Sending* section, we are challenged to go into the world to do God's work. It may include a parting hymn, "Song of Simeon" *(Nunc Dimittis)*, commissioning, benediction, and postlude.

This fourfold design is the basic pattern of worship in many churches where the eucharistic or communion meal is celebrated. Services that do not include communion may take on a simple threefold design: *Gathering, Word,* and *Sending*. Some churches think of the design for services without communion in a different manner. The broad design may include the following elements:

Praise
Preparation
Hearing the Word
Responding to the Word
OR
Gathering
Praising
Confessing
Proclaiming
Sending

Whatever the style of worship, it is important for worship leaders to identify the overall design of the service as the team starts to plan the details.

SHAPE OF WORSHIP

Worship elements within each aspect of the design may vary greatly in mood, energy, length, and volume. As a planning team starts to think about the various elements they want to use in worship, it is important to know where each fits into the overall design of the service. What happens before and after the element? What is the desired mood of that part of the service?

In the Enlivening Worship seminar, the worship teams listed adjectives to describe the various moods of worship. Each mood is appropriate to inspirational and life-transforming worship. We divided the moods into two groups: moods of high energy and moods of low energy. Here is how participants described the two categories.

Moods of High Energy	Moods of Low Energy
• Triumphant	• Meditative
• Exuberant	• Pensive
• Joyful	• Contemplative
• Happy	• Mournful
• Boisterous	• Somber
• Intense	• Reflective
• Celebratory	• Thoughtful
• Glorious	• Penitential
• Loud	• Soft
• Fast	• Slow

Let's go back to the model service, "Waiting for the Light." Under the broad category *Listening*, there are eight worship sections: breathing, song, drama 1, song, drama 2, song, drama 3, and song. Under the heading *Responding*, there are seven elements: invitation to confession, silence, assurance, song and lighting of candles, prayer, song, and silence. The seminar participants graded the energy level of each event from zero to ten. (Zero represented silence and ten the highest energy level.) We then put our data on a graph, so we could see the shape of the service. On the *x* axis, we listed the worship events from left to right in the order they occurred in the service. This functioned as a timeline for the service. On the *y* axis, we marked the energy level of each event with a dot. By connecting the dots, we could easily see the shape of the service as a whole, involving many interdependent parts.

Waiting for the Light

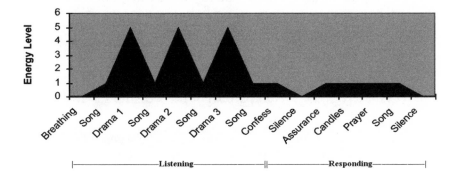

WORSHIP ELEMENTS

After seeing the graph, the seminar participants discussed contrasting elements of the service. There was an obvious distinction between the two major sections. The *Listening* part exerted much more energy, while the *Responding* section was calmer and more contemplative. Within each section, they noticed an internal scheme. The repetition of the meditative song "Wait for the Lord" helped unify the first section. The dramas, with elements of anxiety, tension, and even humor, provided a strong contrast to the song. This internal scheme of the listening section may be represented by the following letters:

A   B   A   B   A   B   A

A represents the first element (the song), and B a contrasting worship element (drama). The musicians at the seminar noted that this logical format is the same as the rondo form in music. As stated in the music appreciation book *The Enjoyment of Music,* "In all the arts a balance is required between unity and variety, symmetry and asymmetry, activity and repose. Repetition fixes the material in our mind and satisfies the need for the familiar, while contrast stimulates our interest and feeds our desire for change."[4] The internal scheme of the *Responding* section may also be represented in letters. The confession was a new worship element, and is thus represented by the letter C. Another event, the lighting of candles, accompanied by a new song, was given the letter D. By returning to the first song of the service, a sense of the familiar was achieved. This return is represented by the letter A. Here is the overall pattern of the worship service.

1. *Listening*   2. *Responding*

A   B   A   B   A   B   A   C   D   A

Each worship service will take on its own unique shape. Sometimes the graph may not have many elements of contrast. For example, a service in the Taize tradition will not have many high points. Each element is hushed and calm, so the shape may look more like a slow ascending and descending arc.

Here is the shape of a Morning Prayer service we had at the Enlivening Worship seminar. It contained more elements of contrast and *fewer repetitive parts.*

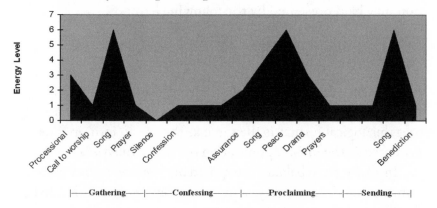

WORSHIP ELEMENTS

Charting the service in this manner helps members of the worship team see how the individual aspects of worship relate to the whole. As team members lead a part in worship, they must think how the element fits into the overall design. They must know what is happening before and after the event to understand the desired energy level. Those involved in music will need to think of the energy level of a song or piece in terms of the following elements:

+ *Dynamics*—the relative volume
+ *Tempo*—the speed
+ *Pitch*—the highness or lowness of sound; frequency
+ *Timbre*—the characteristics of the sound

Similar considerations may be made for those involved in reading or drama. We recommend that those participating in congregational reading or drama mark the text and practice with the following factors in mind:

+ *Volume*—the degree of loudness or softness
+ *Pace*—the speed at which one speaks
+ *Inflections*—the rising and falling of the voice
+ *Color*—the voice quality (bright, dark, thin, heavy, nasal, relaxed, intense, etc.)

When worship teams look at the shape of a service, they should keep several important factors in mind. The shape of a service is influenced by the season of the church year and the theme of the day. More penitential seasons, such as Advent and Lent, are generally lower on the energy-level axis. On the other hand, seasons of rejoicing, like Christmas and Easter, have a higher energy level than seasons of penitence and preparation. Most services need a balance between high and low energy levels. If a service has too many successive events at the low level, worshipers may become inattentive. When a service has only high energy levels, one may miss out on the fullness of God's story. In our worship we need time for exuberant praise as well as time to hear the still small voice.

FLOW IN WORSHIP

The manner in which worship events are connected affects the flow of a service. As worship teams think about the shape of a service, they need to look at how the elements are linked together. What makes events flow in a logical manner? What makes events seem disconnected? Does an event need a transition? These questions may be difficult for some teams to answer because worship planning is subjective. It is important to remember that people perceive beauty and learn in multiple ways. To assist the worship team in this process, we devised four methods by which events may be linked.

Linking Parts of Worship with One Another

The connection of parts of the service needs to be thought through carefully. Joining events of similar moods may help to unify a section of worship. However, linking too many like events together may leave worshipers thinking that the service is boring and static. Certain services, like a meditative Evening Prayer, may purposely have a succession of quiet, reflective events. On the other hand, the joining of contrasting elements may give the section interest and variety. Linking strongly contrasting events can appear jolting and disruptive. At times the flow of a service may be intentionally jarring, however.

Daryl recalls a powerful use of abruptness in the flow of the Tenebrae service (Service of Shadows) on a Good Friday evening at St. Peter's. This service portrays the emotional aspects of the Passion story through readings and music. After each reading a candle is extinguished, and the sanctuary becomes darker. Finally, after the cantor chants Psalm 22, which Jesus quoted on the cross, the Christ candle is extinguished, and the sanctuary is cast into darkness. A large bell is tolled thirty-three times to represent the years of Christ's life. After the tolling, the worshipers sit in total silence and darkness. After the period of silence, a musician violently beats a drum at full volume. The effect is shocking. This sudden noise depicts the earthquake at the time of Christ's death. People sometimes gasp as they come to grips with the horrible death and sacrifice of the Savior. In this case, moving suddenly from zero to ten on the energy level has a purpose. Many worshipers sit for a long time in silence, having been moved to tears.

Linking Events with Pauses

Sometimes a pause is needed between two worship events. This is easily done simply by inserting a moment of silence. Taking time in worship to ponder and reflect is an effective way of encouraging a sense of God's presence in worship. Worship leaders should not hurry from one event to the next but should allow time for the full impact of worship to sink into our being. At St. Peter's we pray silently at several points in the service. During the confession, we allow a quiet moment for each worshiper to acknowledge his or her shortcomings before God. This pause in worship enhances our awareness of our sins and prepares us for encountering the Holy in the next part of the service.

Another valuable use of silence is for meditation after the sermon. When we first tried this at St. Peter's, some people became fidgety, thinking the organist had fallen asleep during the sermon. We soon realized that worshipers felt more comfortable if we included a suggestion in the bulletin that they take time to reflect on what God is saying to us. Sometimes the word of God spoken through the sermon is so powerful that jumping right into a hymn would seem disruptive to the mood and message. Silence is now a common practice at St. Peter's. The worshipers settle in during these silent times to allow God to speak to them through these powerful pauses in worship.

Certain sounds may also be used as pauses between elements of worship. Simple instruments such as wind chimes, gong, singing bowl, bells, rain sticks, hand chimes, or drums may enhance the desired mood during these pauses. Instruments used in this manner should not play a song or piece of music, but rather should be sounded freely to create a pause rather than announce a new event. Try using wind chimes or rain sticks between the prayers of petition during Lent or Advent. These ethereal sounds will create a contemplative mood for the prayers.

Linking Events with Music

When many spoken worship events occur in succession, it is sometimes wise to interject music. Daryl recalls hearing worshipers say, "I cannot stay focused when I hear four Scripture passages in a row. My mind needs a break." Music is a powerful tool to reinforce the spoken word with additional meaning and emotion. Sometimes an anthem may complement one of the Scripture passages. In some liturgical churches, the assembly welcomes the Gospel reading with sung acclamations, a sung alleluia, or another appropriate song.

Music during the prayers is another powerful tool to get people actively involved in the act of worship. This is a dynamic tradition in many African American churches. Try using Ken Medema's song "Lord, Listen to Your Children Praying" as a prayer response. At the conclusion of each petition, have the assembly sing the song prayerfully. The keyboard player may continue to improvise softly during the petitions and then play the last phrase as the introduction when the leader says, "God, hear our prayer." Daryl recalls the first time he used this technique in worship. It was at a Lutheran church, and the petitions were many that day. "I thought for sure people would be upset because the prayer time was much longer than usual with the additional music." He was shocked when he heard comments such as these:

"It seemed like we were all involved in the prayers."

"There was an added emotion to the prayers that I can't describe."

"We were participants, not just observers."

We recognize that playing softly may make the music difficult to hear for those who are hearing impaired. Accordingly, we encourage you to experiment with volume, both to preserve the contemplative experience and to include worshipers with hearing loss.

At St. Peter's we use music at various places in the service, depending on the mood and theme of the day. Sometimes we use music during the Call to Worship, Invocation, Confession, Sermon, Prayers, Communion, or Benediction. Many times worship planners get into a rut by thinking they can have music only in certain parts of the service. We encourage small congregations to look at new ways of using music. Music has great power to bring fresh meaning to a traditional part of the liturgy.

Linking Events with Words

Sometimes parts of worship need transitional words to help the flow of the service. At the beginning of the service, after announcements are made, we need to invite the congregation to move toward a more receptive and worshipful attitude. At St. Peter's the pastor says right before the prelude, "Let us prepare our hearts for worship." He or she then proceeds to the altar for a time of silence, thus inviting the congregation to prepare prayerfully for worship.

Words are used in calling the congregation to confession. Sometimes these are printed in the bulletin, and sometimes

they are just spoken. Although it is important to include helpful rubrics in the bulletin, sometimes the spoken word is more
appropriate. For example, when the worship leader is trying to
establish a particular mood in the service, he or she may model
it in speech. In times like this, it is important to pay attention
to the timbre of the voice. Just by speaking loudly or softly, the
leader will guide the change in mood. On the other hand, you
may find that the spoken word interrupts the flow of the service and that printed words are more suitable.

We have also found transitional words helpful after the
passing of the peace. At St. Peter's this is an important time for
welcoming one another and is often boisterous as worshipers
move all around. In a small church, it seems like a family get-
together, and people make sure that visitors are greeted. The
pastor calls the assembly back to quietness after the peace by
saying something like this: "We invite you to continue your fellowship time after the service. We will have refreshments for
everyone in the social hall, which is located on level 1." This announcement actually does two things. It reminds congregants
of the social hour and informs visitors of the opportunity, while
calling people back to worship.

Introductions to the reading of Scripture can be a powerful
means of alerting people to wake up and hear the word of God.
We encourage the lectors to begin with a simple introduction of
the text, often putting it in the context of the book. For example,
before a lament from the book of Psalms, the reader might say,
"This psalm is believed to have been written by David after he
had sinned grievously against God. Hear his words of sorrow
for what he has done." Sometimes "Hear now the word of God"
is a phrase used before the readings. At the conclusion of the
Gospel lesson, a phrase such as "Holy words, holy wisdom" is
sometimes spoken as a sign that the reading has ended.

One of the joys of being in a small congregation is the intimacy of the pastor and congregants. The pastor at St. Peter's often comes to the center of the sanctuary and recites the
Scriptures from memory or portrays them through drama. She

looks right into the eyes of the congregants and at the conclusion of the Scripture will say, "Let us meditate on these words to see what God is saying to us." A period of silence then follows as she makes her way to the pulpit.

Sometimes a Call to Offering is printed in the bulletin, but if not, it is appropriate to invite worshipers verbally to bring their gifts, perhaps with the use of a Scripture passage that highlights the relationship between God's generosity and our own ability to give. In our service, it usually follows the Lord's Prayer, so a transition is needed. As mentioned previously, there is a mood change here—from meditation and intercession to celebration. The shift can seem abrupt if the offering is received quickly without a connecting event. On occasion the pastor at St. Peter's will provide a statement that relates to the prayer she has just led. For example, she may turn us from asking for God's care to giving love to God with this phrase: "We can rejoice because God has heard our cries and answers our prayers. Let us now give our love back to God for all we have received. Bring your gifts with joy." The tone of her voice, her smile, and the joy she interjects into this phrase lead the people to a new event. Still, it is important for pastors to remember that an abundance of words in the flow of worship may detract from some worshipers' experiences. Accordingly, pastors and worship leaders need to plan their words carefully, following the adage that "less is more."

In conclusion, to have well crafted worship services it is important that worship leaders spend considerable time thinking and planning services with a logical and meaningful design, an interesting yet unifying shape, and a flow that smoothly connects worship events. Following the process described in this chapter will help the team maintain its focus in worship planning. We recommend that teams remember their primary purpose—to help people meet and worship the Divine. When this is at the forefront of their thinking, it will be easier for each person to come to the planning sessions in a spirit of love and humility and with an open and creative mind.

ENLIVENING WORSHIP IN YOUR CHURCH

Take a half-day retreat with your worship team. Spend time in prayer asking God to inspire and guide the process of developing vital and meaningful worship. Evaluate several of your most recent worship services as they relate to design, shape, and flow, considering the following points.

Design

- Determine the design of the services.
- Is the design the same or different for each service?
- If the sections are not clearly defined, discuss ways you might improve on the design.
- Discuss the benefits of having the major headings listed in the bulletin.

Shape

- Take the most recent worship service, and list the worship events in the order they occurred in the service.
- Beside each event, put a number from zero to ten (zero is silence, and ten is the highest energy imaginable) to represent the energy level for that element.
- Chart the shape of your services, using the service "Waiting for the Light" as a model. List events on the x axis, and plot the energy levels on the y axis.
- Discuss the logic and impact of that shape. Are there areas that felt stagnant and boring? Were there elements that were too sudden and jarring? Was there a balance between unifying and contrasting events?
- Discuss ways you could improve the shape of the service.

Flow

+ How were events connected in the service (succession, pauses, music, words)?
+ Are there times when you need better connectors to help the flow?
+ Discuss how the various events were executed by the worship leaders. In what ways can the worship leaders better match the desired energy levels?
+ List your areas of strengths and weaknesses in the flow of the worship service.
+ Make a plan to include strengths and eliminate weaknesses in your future worship services.

CHAPTER 8

THEOLOGY FOR THE CHURCH MUSICIAN

PARTNERS IN SPIRITUAL FORMATION

WHENEVER BRUCE TELLS a group of laypeople, "You are all theologians," he is usually met with chuckles or looks of skepticism as if to say, "Who, me? A theologian? That's just for Ph.D.'s!" But Bruce then explains, "Whenever we ask questions about the meaning of our lives, the nature of the world in which we live, the reasons for suffering, the quest for hope in difficult times, or the reality of answered and unanswered prayers, we are asking some of the most important theological questions." After offering that summary, he is typically met with knowing glances and nodding heads. A theologian, and the theologian in each one of us, asks "big questions"—questions about God and creation, and life and death—whether in the complex and sophisticated language of magi or the simple and straightforward phrases of shepherds. The two of us believe that theology is not just the province of seminary professors or people who write books; all Christians are called to be theologians—that is, to seek to love God with their minds and to articulate their understanding of God and human life in healthy and life-affirming ways.

While the two of us believe that every congregational pastor, or minister of Word and Sacrament, is called to be the primary public theologian of her or his congregation, we equally affirm that every member, regardless of her or his age, has a theological vocation to grow in faith and understanding of God's presence in the world. The Gospels declare that Jesus grew in "wisdom and stature"—and so should we! Accordingly, in this chapter, we hope to provide a pathway to basic theological reflection as a way of helping church musicians in partnership with pastors and congregations become more theologically insightful. We will not attempt to be comprehensive, but we want to help congregational musicians think theologically in the selection of music as well as in their instruction of choirs and worship leadership. In so doing, church musicians and their worshiping communities will grow in wisdom, stature, and faithfulness to God through participating in meaningful and life-changing worship.

As we stated earlier, theological reflection cannot be avoided. The question is whether the way we express our theology will hurt or help our brothers and sisters in Christ. Some twenty-five years ago, Bruce was surprised at the theological wisdom hidden in a question asked by his then four-year-old son Matt. After father and son had read from a book of Christmas stories each night in the week before the Christmas celebration, Matt asked Bruce, "If Joseph was Jesus's father, was God his grandfather?" Without knowing it, this young child touched some of the key issues involving Jesus's humanity and relationship to God that inspired the writing of the Apostles' and Nicene Creeds. This same spirit of theological inquiry, often a matter of spiritual life and death for congregants and for us, emerges in conversations with patients in hospital rooms or family members following an unexpected natural disaster or car accident. Pastors and laypeople alike ask questions such as "Where was God during Hurricane Katrina?" "Was 9/11 really God's punishment of the United States for its greed and immorality?" "Why was I spared in the accident, when my brother died?" These theological questions are as old as the book of Job and as current as today's evening news. In light of the universality of theological reflection, every faithful Christian is called to respond to the following questions:

- Will you be a thoughtful or a superficial theologian?
- Will your theological explanations encourage understanding or close off further questioning?
- Will you settle for simplistic explanations of life's most challenging issues? Or will you ask hard questions of yourself, your pastor, and God?
- Will your theological descriptions of God's role in sickness, traumatic experiences, or injustice bring healing to people in pain or further blame the victims of tragedies for their suffering?

The two of us believe that church musicians should pursue theological education as a part of their vocation as worship leaders. Many church musicians regularly meet with the congregation's pastor or lay worship committee to plan worship services and to choose anthems, hymns, and songs related to the Scriptures of the day or the seasons of the Christian year. As pivotal participants in creating lively and meaningful congregational worship services, church musicians are challenged to be theologically thoughtful and astute in selecting hymns and anthems as well as in guiding the flow of the worship service. They are also called to prepare themselves to respond appropriately to theological issues that emerge in their encounters with choir members and worship participants of all ages. Although the church musician most regularly deals with the congregation's pastor, choir, and worship committee, he or she also helps shape the theology of those who attend worship by his or her choice of hymns, anthems, preludes, and postludes.

Throughout this book, the two of us have noted the importance of hymns, songs, and anthems in spiritual formation and theological education, whether among laypeople, church musicians, or pastors. In many ways, what we sing shapes our faith.

When we sing, we not only "pray twice"; we also "think twice" as hymns repeated year after year shape our understanding of God and our response to the tragedies of life. If you want to change a faith community's approach to theology or mission, you need to transform the style and content of its hymns and songs as well as its sermons. Accordingly, as we've said before, pastors and church musicians need to be as theologically astute in selecting hymns and music as they are in preparing sermons or the order of worship.

Daryl and Bruce have on numerous occasions heard testimonies to the power of music to transform a congregation's life and theology. A Maryland pastor recounts how learning music of other cultures through hymns and chants from Asia, Africa, and First Nations America awakened her congregation to a new sense of mission.

> Our congregation began to see these "strangers" as Christian brothers and sisters. I provided brief explanations for each new hymn, and once or twice I brought in photographs of Christians worshiping in Africa, Asia, or on Native American reservations, and this made all the difference in the world. My very traditional German congregation now sees its worship as connected with the global Christian movement.

Another pastor recalls a conversation with one of her parishioners, who reported that paying closer attention to the words of the hymns sung in worship challenged her previous theological assumptions.

> While the cross of Christ is still central to my faith, I'm struggling with my childhood images of atonement. I wonder if all those hymns about the blood of Christ and the need for God to sacrifice his Son really help us understand how much God loves us. Did Jesus really have to die for God to forgive our sins? Did God compel Jesus to die in order to be able to love

us? I don't have an answer, and that's OK. Maybe Jesus saves us in ways I can't fully understand.

After singing and reading through many of the inclusive-language revisions in *The New Century Hymnal* of the United Church of Christ, another fairly traditional congregant asserted:

> While I'm not always happy with the changed language in traditional hymns, I've come to realize that God can be described in many ways, not just as a Father. At first, I wasn't comfortable with the new words in hymns like "Good Christian Friends, Rejoice." But, now I recognize that for some people, "friends" more accurately includes women as well as men.

CHURCH MUSICIANS AS CONGREGATIONAL THEOLOGIANS

Week after week, church musicians help shape a congregation's approach to worship. Whether the congregation's liturgy is formal or informal, one task of the church musician is to remind the congregation of the times and seasons of the Christian year and of the important role music plays in deepening our faith. Even the most informal Pentecostal or "emerging" Christian worship service will, over the course of a year, implicitly repeat the cycle of Advent and Christmas and Holy Week and Easter, not to mention the celebration of Pentecost and the Lenten season.

During his workshops on enlivening worship and music, Daryl recommends that church musicians look for ways to show how the music of a particular season can enhance its theological implications. During Advent, Daryl and Pastor Bonnie Hollinger, his wife, offered a four-week adult forum class at St. Peter's United Church of Christ on the music of Advent.

Together they led the participants on a journey through this season of waiting by focusing on music and the arts. Congregants noted that it was a wonderful time to think theologically about the celebration of the Christian church through various Advent traditions. Members of the group shared their own traditions of celebrating Advent and reflected on the mystery of some Advent traditions the church observes.

They sang a diversity of Advent songs—some familiar and some new. They sang and studied songs from Africa, Latin America, and Native America, as well as from the Geneva Psalter and the classical era, plus early American tunes and contemporary songs. As they sang music from other times and places, they experienced the varied ways Christians celebrate Advent. They pondered the music of the songs as it related to the theology of the texts. Some of the participants acknowledged that they were often frustrated because they didn't get to sing Christmas carols during Advent. Others confessed that before they took the class, they hadn't given much thought to the theological and spiritual importance of waiting during Advent. Still others were surprised how the quiet, reflective music helped enhance the meaning of the words. It proved to be a valuable time in which all attending—laypeople, pastor, and musicians—were given an opportunity to be theologians. Beyond that, pastor and church musician, Bonnie and Daryl, both gained from their study and preparation new theological and historical insights related to the traditions and music of Advent.

Church musicians are teachers. They often select hymns and anthems, direct and teach choirs of all ages, and work with congregational musicians (handbell choirs, high-school trumpet players and flutists). Although church musicians serving small congregations rarely receive seminary training, it is imperative for them to take theological reflection seriously. We believe that reflection on the traditional creeds of the church as well as contemporary denominational creeds can be a helpful vehicle for the theological education of church musicians. Accordingly, in the following section, while we address the importance of theological reflection for musicians, we recognize that every Christian can likewise learn to think theologically. In the following pages, we invite you to reflect on theological issues raised by the major Christian doctrines related to the nature of the triune God and God's work in the world. This material can be used for either personal or group theological reflection.

THE FAITH WE AFFIRM

As we begin this section, we invite you to go to the section on Christian creeds or affirmations of faith in your congregation's hymnal or another resource. Read meditatively and prayerfully the Apostles' and Nicene Creeds as well as some more contemporary or denominationally based affirmations of faith. Prayerfully meditate on the meaning of these creeds for your life and the life of your congregation. What aspects of the creeds resonate with your experience? What aspects raise theological problems for you or seem irrelevant to Christians and seekers today? How might you rephrase certain creedal statements to creatively address the needs or values of people in your community?

While we recognize that many congregations do not use ancient or contemporary creeds or affirmations of faith as part of their public worship services or in baptismal or membership classes, nevertheless the historic as well as the contemporary creeds of the church teach a theology in miniature to clergy and laypeople alike. Even when they have questions or theological problems about certain aspects of the creeds, most Christians recognize that the historic creeds reflect the central questions of Christian faith.

Among indigenous Australians, "songlines" are traditional songs that enable aboriginal people to navigate Australia's bush country, often finding their way home through uncharted territories. The historic creeds as well as their contemporary companions create the songlines of Christian theology and worship by presenting a vision of reality that guides our path and gives us hope as we face the challenges and possibilities of the present and the unfolding future.

The God We Worship

Reflection on the creeds reminds us that regardless of our theological perspective, Christian theology and worship begin with the praise of God. Christian faith is trinitarian (focused on the dynamic complexity of the Living God), theocentric (God-centered), and doxological (oriented toward gratitude and praise for God's loving care for us and all creation). The Apostles' Creed, whose origins may be as early as the second century, begins with the words "I believe in God, the Father almighty, creator of heaven and earth." In its ancient companion, the fourth-century Nicene Creed, Christians proclaim boldly, "We believe in one God, the Father, the Almighty, maker of heaven and earth, of all that is, seen and unseen." Even more contemporary creeds such as the Affirmation of Faith from the Anglican Church in Aotearoa, New Zealand, and Polynesia center our faith on God's lively and creative presence in the world.

> You, O God, are supreme and holy.
> You create our world and give us life.
> Your purpose overarches everything we do.
> You have always been with us.
> You are God.
> You, O God, are infinitely generous,
> good beyond all measure.
> You came to us before we came to you. . . .[1]

We typically begin the order of worship, as well as our hymnals, with hymns of praise and thanksgiving. Beginning with praise orients us toward the One God "in whom we live and move and have our being" (Acts 17:28). These hymns remind us that we owe our existence in its entirety to our relationship with God, whose creative wisdom and intimate love guide the movements of galaxies, planets, and people alike. Yet in the course of our lives, the doctrine of God as Creator and Parent/ Father is often as much a problem as a comfort for thoughtful Christians, especially when we seek to explain the relationship between divine wisdom and power and the realities of personal and corporate tragedy, sexism, and political oppression.

In the United Church of Christ's *New Century Hymnal,* the presence of "alternative" and "inclusive" versions of the Nicene and Apostles' Creeds represents the emerging recognition that words about God can exclude as well as include, and harm as well as heal, especially as these words relate to gender and sexual identity. So the alternative version of the Apostles' Creed begins, "I believe in God the Father-Mother almighty, creator of heaven and earth."[2] Yet even the attempt to be inclusive raises deep questions of faith, not only as they relate to the gender and imagery of God, the nature of the Trinity, and baptismal language, but also in relationship to the nature of God's power and presence in the ongoing history of the universe.

Pause a moment to consider: What might the word *almighty* mean to a parent whose child has just been killed in an automobile accident? What do the words *maker of heaven and earth* mean when we ponder the culture wars raging around evolutionary theory, intelligent design, and contemporary science? Do you believe that God determines all the important events of life *without our input,* as evangelical leader Rick Warren suggests, or does God desire a world that creatively balances freedom and predictability? How do you speak of God's power and care when you are responding to choir members who have just experienced the death of a close relative or who are facing life-threatening illness? Do you believe that your words on such occasions are helpful? Would you like to explore new ways of speaking about God?

While church musicians are not called to be the primary resident theologians of their congregations, questions of God's activity in our lives may emerge when choir members really listen to the words of congregational hymns and choral anthems. As you consider the theological songlines drawn by your images of God, we ask you to pause again for a moment to consider the following questions: When you were a child, how did you visualize God? Was your image of God abstract, or did your image of God resemble a human being in important ways? How have your images of God changed over the years? What words for God do you use when you pray privately or publicly? These are important questions for pastors and congregants as well as for church musicians.

Because choir members often come to church fresh from dealing with painful personal issues, church musicians need to recognize that theological reflection is essential to their implicit vocation as pastoral caregivers who are called to reflect God's love in worship and music. From a pastoral perspective, you might consider how you respond to questions of divine power and presence, such as: What role does God have in natural disasters or human-initiated tragedies? Where was God in Katrina, in the Christmas tsunami, or in the terrorist acts of 9/11? Where is God present, if at all, in our experiences of disease and pain?

Reflecting on the theological language used by pastors and other members of the Christian community, you might also consider the following questions: When have you experienced God being invoked in ways that have hurt people? When have you observed people speaking of God in ways that have been a source of comfort, hope, inspiration, and positive challenge in your life?

Hymns that Reflect Our Community's Faith

Perhaps, closer to home, you might reflect on whether the hymns and anthems used in worship adequately and accurately reflect the faith of your congregation, especially as these hymns relate to the nature of God's role in the world as well as in the dynamics of personal and congregational life. Do the hymns and music used in worship challenge the congregation to imagine God in new and helpful ways? Do they encourage hopeful action or passive acceptance in relationship to the evils of our time?

After a full day of workshops, a musician came to Daryl and told her story. Pat was a pastoral musician in a small church in Western Pennsylvania. She related that the pastor and the church where she worked were progressive in theology and had a strong emphasis on peace and justice. The church, however, was struggling with decreasing membership and declining participation in the morning service, so the pastor and church leaders decided that they needed a contemporary service to attract new members. They hired an additional musician to lead a praise band for the contemporary service. The whole mood of the service changed. Soon new members were coming to the church, and everyone seemed to be happy with the success of the project. Many members were excited at the signs of growth in the congregation and believed that God was blessing their work.

The honeymoon, however, was short-lived. The service in general attracted a different type of worshiper. The language of the songs used in the contemporary service seemed exclusive and individualistic to many of the older members who valued their mission of peace and justice. Many of the new members used solely male language to refer to God and humankind, a practice that was offensive to some members. Soon the two camps were at odds with each other. Many members started leaving the church because of the theological differences. The pastor was frustrated, because the inclusive and justice-centered gospel she was preaching from the pulpit was undermined by the individualistic and otherworldly songs that were sung by the praise band.

In seeking to respond to the worship conflicts in this congregation, Daryl asked Pat about the process the church had gone through in deciding to begin a service of this nature. Pat replied sadly that little thought or communication had taken place. Any discussion about the music centered on style and not theology. The congregation learned a valuable, but costly lesson—the importance for pastors, church musicians, and congregants to use music that represents the theology and mission of their church.

Theology matters, whether in pulpit, choir loft, or pew. If your congregation were suddenly transported back to the seventeenth century, would the hymns and liturgy characteristic of your congregational worship fit in or seem out of place? (Although we treasure the "old, old story" of faith, you would surely notice some dissonance between your current worship service and that of the first North American settlers!) While the songlines of faith can never be fully comprehended, nevertheless, as we look in a mirror dimly, we can still glimpse images of God that enable us to grow in personal stature, respond to suffering, and support people in crisis in ways appropriate to our time and place.

The Christ We Worship

What we think about Jesus matters in our worship and congregational life. In most Christian creeds, the second affirmation of faith involves the person and work of Jesus Christ, our Healer, Teacher, and Savior. The Apostles' Creed proclaims, "I believe in Jesus Christ, his only Son, our Lord," and then, along with the Nicene Creed, describes his unique birth, saving work, death and resurrection, and heavenly glory. The United Church of Christ Statement of Faith affirms, "In Jesus Christ, the man of Nazareth, our crucified and risen Savior, you have come to us and shared our common lot, conquering sin and death, and reconciling the world to yourself."[3]

The life and work of Jesus in bringing wholeness to the world will always go beyond what we can imagine or describe. Like all other affirmations of faith, our words about Jesus point beyond themselves to a mystery that transforms our lives but cannot be limited by creed or doctrine. As John's Gospel reminds us, "There are also many other things that Jesus did; if every one of them were written down, I suppose that the world itself could not contain the books that would be written" (John 21:25). Still, we must recognize that our understanding of Jesus is important as we respond to the needs of our congregations and our own deepest questions of faith.

Theologically astute—and particularly not-so-astute—church musicians are challenged to reflect on their own theological understanding of Jesus of Nazareth. You might consider questions such as the following: What is your favorite Gospel story, and why? What does your choice of a favorite Gospel story tell you about your understanding of Jesus? We invite you to compare the descriptions of Jesus's birth and resurrection found in the four Gospels. How are they similar? How do they differ in content and focus? How do you understand the differences among the Gospels in their descriptions of Jesus's birth, resurrection, or other events in Jesus's life? What are the theological implications of the early church's acceptance of four different stories, the four Gospels, in describing the significance of Jesus's life? Does it matter that only two of the Gospels—Matthew and Luke—describe Jesus's birth? How might this diversity among the Gospels shape our own response to theological diversity within the church today?

As you consider the religious and ethnic pluralism of our time, take time to reflect on the following theological questions: What does it mean for us to say that Jesus is God's "only Son," and how does our affirmation of Jesus's unique relationship to God shape our attitude toward other faith traditions? If Jesus reveals God's true nature, what does this say about God's relationship with humankind, especially people of other faiths or of no faith tradition at all? How does the truth that we find in Jesus relate to the "truths" of other religious traditions? What happens in this life and the next to those who do not proclaim Jesus as their Savior? Are there specific theological or doctrinal words that we need to use to become true followers of Jesus or, as some Christians say, to be saved? While we can never fully answer these and other questions related to the impact of Jesus on our lives and the world, our willingness to reflect on them with an open spirit is a sign of our willingness to grow in our own faith as well as to creatively engage in dialogue with congregants and people beyond the church who have different understandings of Jesus's life and the scope of salvation.

We recognize that theologians have pondered these questions for two thousand years without full agreement or a clear understanding of Jesus's identity and relationship to other faith traditions. Although our understanding of Jesus, like our understanding of God, will always remain limited, still we cannot avoid questions about Jesus in the course of choosing music or relating to choir members. Every so often, a choir practice turns into a theological discussion. Occasionally, as the hymnals are put away until Sunday's worship service, a member may express her struggle to understand God's attitude toward other faiths or the nature of the cross and how that reflects the relationship of God the Creator and Jesus the Redeemer. While we realize that you as pastor or church musician may not have all the answers, your calling as a congregational leader mandates your willingness to listen and to share your faith in ways that deepen choir members' understanding of God's presence in Jesus's life as well as your own faith. When you, as church musician, respond to the questions or viewpoints of others, don't think that you need to have all the answers, and remember that you can always invite choir members to seek the guidance of the pastor.

Spirit-filled Song

The Apostles' Creed simply notes, "I believe in the Holy Spirit." Later, the Nicene Creed proclaimed, "We believe in the Holy Spirit, the Lord, the giver of Life, who proceeds from the Father and the Son." The more contemporary creed of the United Church of Canada proclaims that we believe in God "who works in us and others by the Holy Spirit." The Statement of Faith of the United Church of Christ affirms, "You [God] bestow upon us your Holy Spirit, creating and renewing the Church of Jesus Christ, binding in covenant faithful people of all ages, tongues, and races." While there are diverse understandings of the work of the Holy Spirit, most Christians see the Holy Spirit as God's immanent, uniting, and inspiring presence in our lives and in the life and worship of the church. Sadly, many mainstream Christians identify the movements of God's Spirit only with the dramatic worship of Pentecostal Christians and televangelists. They forget that the spirit that burns brightly in Pentecostal worship also glows in their own less dramatic times of worship. The Holy Spirit may descend upon us with tongues and fire (Acts 2:1–13); it may also come to us in a gentle life-giving breath (John 20:22). The Holy Spirit may even inspire us in moments of quiet prayer and contemplation in "sighs too deep for words" (Rom. 8:26).

As church musicians reflect on the works of the Spirit in their congregation, they are called to remember their own experiences of God's Spirit, whether in moments of inspiration or reconciliation. To understand more deeply the presence of God's Spirit in their congregations, they might consider questions such as these:

- Where is the Holy Spirit present in the world?
- Is it restricted to the church or is it global in impact?
- Where have you experienced the Spirit's movements in your life and in your worship?
- How can we become more open to the movements of the Holy Spirit in our worship and congregational life?

Church musicians can also remind their choir members that God is present in their choir and in their congregation, regardless of its size. In the spirit of the visioning process of appreciative inquiry, church musicians can ask both choir members and congregants questions such as these: "When did you feel most inspired in worship? When have you felt God's nearness in worship or in daily life? Where have you experienced God's unexpected blessing in your life?"[4] This process may inspire choir members to explore new ways to be faithful to God in their singing and worship. In discovering the Spirit's presence in their small choir, choir singers may experience a sense of renewal, possibility, and openness to new movements of God in church.

The identification of the Holy Spirit with the breath of God inspires church musicians, choir members, and the congregation as a whole to experience the simple act of breathing, so central to the sung voice, as a manifestation of God's presence in our lives. Our worship would truly be enlivened if we could imagine God breathing through us, filling us with new life, whenever we gather for worship.

PAYING ATTENTION TO THEOLOGY IN CHOIR PRACTICE

One of the vocations of church musicians, like pastors, is to inspire the encounter with God through the interplay of words and music. Daryl encourages choir directors to talk about how the music enhances the text of the hymns and anthems used during choir rehearsal. He likes to use one of the hymns or anthems as a catalyst for a devotional time at the beginning of each choir rehearsal. It sets the tone for the rehearsal and encourages musicians to think more deeply about the music they are about to sing. Rehearsals need to be about much more than just singing the correct notes at the right time. Choir practice involves members engaging in the theological reflection as well as preparation for Sunday's anthem.

Daryl recalls one instance that demonstrates how the choir's reflection on Scripture and music led to a teaching moment. The Gospel lesson was about the ten lepers, and Pastor Bonnie Hollinger's sermon was titled "Praise Changes Things."

The anthem Daryl picked was "Praise, Praise, Praise the Lord!" from Cameroon. In the choir rehearsal before that Sunday, Daryl spent time teaching about the nature of the African song with its layering of different rhythms and voice parts. The choir at first felt a bit uncomfortable with the freedom and flexibility of the song. "You mean we don't know exactly how many times we will sing the song," one of the members complained. In response, Daryl explained the spontaneity and spirited singing of our brothers and sisters in Africa. We have a lot we can learn from the worship in Africa, Daryl noted, as he asked the choir to consider this question: "Does our praise bubble up freely from our inner being, or must we always know where we're going in worship?"

As the choir continued to discuss the theology reflected in the hymn, Daryl noted that in Jesus's encounter with the lepers, the Samaritan was the only one to return to give thanks. Daryl also invited the choir singers to reflect on their own experience: "While it is easy to fault the others for not returning, how often do we get caught up in our own stuff and forget to give thanks to God?" Then, after a few more minutes of dialogue on the nature of gratitude, Daryl offered this prayer:

> God of mystery and wonder, you are with us in the good times and the bad—in times of glory and in times of doubt. As we sing your praise tonight, may we remember to take our song of thanksgiving with us throughout the week. In all the twists and turns that come our way, lead us to praise and thanksgiving. May words of gratitude flow freely from our lips and hearts as we take this song with us this week. In the name of the one who heals and brings us peace, Amen.

Music and Pastoral Care

In the course of the year, church members and choirs, as well as the congregation as a whole, often contemplate matters of life and death. In small churches, the death of a longtime member or a small child can be devastating. Because of their size, small churches cannot hide the harsh realities of life or deny the reality of death and the grief we experience when a beloved congregant dies. Small congregations are reminded of their own fragility and the importance of each person when a member dies or is seriously ill. Members can remain anonymous in large congregations, but in small churches, "if one member suffers, all suffer together with it; if one member is honored, all rejoice together with it" (1 Cor. 12:26).

While church musicians must contend with their own grief in times of loss within the congregation, they can provide solace, courage, and inspiration to choir member and congregant alike by drawing on the great songs of faith. Many of our favorite hymns affirm God's faithfulness. Such hymns embody the Apostles' Creed's hopeful affirmation of "the forgiveness of sins, the resurrection of the body, and life everlasting." With misty eyes, church musicians can lead congregations in faithful praise with songs such as "Great Is Thy Faithfulness," "It Is Well with My Soul," "Precious Lord, Take My Hand," or "My Hope Is Built" (also known as "The Solid Rock").

Theologically sensitive church musicians recognize that they have a pastoral role in moments of grief and loss, both to the choir and to the congregation as a whole, grounded in the power of music and hymnody both to comfort and sustain in times of grief and loss. Accordingly, church musicians need to reflect carefully on the following questions: Are the hymns we sing appropriate to the particular family's life situation and our congregation's theology? Do they comfort and sustain or raise theological questions prematurely and in an inappropriate context? Do these hymns acknowledge the reality of loss while affirming God's fidelity in every season of life? Often our best responses to tragedy occur in the creative partnership of pastors and church musicians.

Music and Mission

Although many more theological questions might be considered in our reflections on the role of the church musician as theologian, we will conclude with a brief reflection on mission. The two of us believe that Christian communities are called to be lights in the world, whose worship deepens our faith and inspires us to mission. Theologically growing church musicians consider the relationship between individual and community and between the congregation and the wider world in the selection of hymns and the conduct of worship. What we do in worship truly matters in the week that follows. While they are often separated in the minds of pastors and laypeople, there is an intimate connection in the life of faith between contemplation and action, worship and service. As one church marquee notes, "Enter to worship, go forth to serve." In this light, church musicians, along with pastors and congregants, need to ask: Are the hymns chosen for worship concerned primarily with individual piety, social concern, or care for the neighbor? Or are they a blend of individual and social well-being? As you consider your congregation's worship, do the worship and music inspire mission to and with the larger community? Does the worship take into consideration the "least of these" in your community and challenge members to live out their faith in the complexities of work, community life, and political involvement?

The two of us believe that vital congregations take theological education seriously and are committed to teaching the ancient and contemporary visions of our faith, whether in an adult study or a preschool class or in the context of choir practice and congregational worship. When church musicians make a commitment to their own theological education, they enable the light of learning to shine brightly in choir practice, in individual conversations, and in the church's public worship.

ENLIVENING WORSHIP AND MUSIC IN YOUR CHURCH

In this chapter's spiritual exercise, we first invite you to spend a few hours reflecting on the hymnal your congregation uses. In the spirit of *lectio divina*, or holy reading, pause reflectively and prayerfully to consider how God is speaking to you within the first lines and words of the hymns.

+ What hymns inspire your faith journey right now?
+ What hymns give you hope and energize you to proclaim the gospel?
+ What hymns raise challenging theological issues for you?
+ In what ways do you experience God in these theological challenges?

Second, take a moment to reflect on the hymns that have shaped your faith as a Christian, both as a child and as an adult. After noting a handful of your favorite hymns, reflect on what insights they give you about your own faith. In light of this reflection, consider whether any important aspects of Christian faith are missing or de-emphasized. What do you think these omissions mean for your identity as a Christian? How might you continue to grow in your understanding of the fullness of Christian faith and experience?

Third, choose one of your favorite hymns and live with that hymn for a week. Read the words of the hymn daily in your home or office. Sing or hum the hymn throughout the day. Use the hymn as a way of recovering your spiritual center when you become anxious or harried in the course of the week. In what way does focusing on the inspiration of a particular hymn change the way you look at the world or respond to events in your daily life? What might it be like to live your life according to the theology of your favorite and most inspiring hymns?

CHAPTER 9

GREAT IS GOD'S FAITHFULNESS

MUSIC AND WORSHIP THROUGH ALL THE SEASONS OF LIFE

THROUGHOUT THIS BOOK, the two of us have affirmed the importance of music and worship in the theological and spiritual formation of Christians and congregational life. We sing our faith, and our hymns and songs create the theological and spiritual songlines of our lives. Hymns, songs, and liturgies shape what we see, our attitudes toward change and diversity, our responses to the unexpected and anticipated challenges of life. The songs we proclaim in worship transform our lives, individually and congregationally, and give us courage to face life's most difficult challenges. Worship is a primary factor in the creation of what practical theologian Craig Dykstra describes as the ecclesial imagination, "a way of seeing and being that emerges when a community of faith, together as a community, comes increasingly to share the knowledge of God and to live a way of abundant life—not only in church but also in the many contexts where they live their lives."[1]

In the course of this book, we have invoked "all season" hymns and songs such as "Great Is Thy Faithfulness," "How Can I Keep from Singing?" and "Blest Be the Tie That Binds." These and many other hymns of faith remind us that a song in our hearts and a hymn on our minds can enable us and our communities to face unimaginable and inescapable pain, grief, and loss with grace, courage, and dignity. Ours is a resurrection faith, but new life often comes through faithfully facing the pain and abandonment of Good Friday and Holy Saturday, when we, like Jesus's first disciples, face the future, not knowing whether there will be a resurrection, healing, or happy ending for us or for the people and institutions to which we are dedicated. Faithful music and worship enable us to embrace without denial personal and communal tragedy in light of God's all-encompassing and all-creative faithfulness and love.

Whenever we are tempted to think that our parents in the faith faced fewer challenges in affirming their faith than we do, we need only remember the words of "Faith of Our Fathers," which can be updated with words such as "martyrs" or "parents" for our more inclusive age.

> Faith of our fathers! living still in spite of dungeon, fire, and
> sword;
> O how our hearts beat high with joy, whene'er we hear that
> glorious word!
> Faith of our fathers, holy faith! We will be true to thee till
> death.[2]

Our parents in the faith could not escape the tragedies of life, nor can we. Indeed, the first Christians faced persecution, imprisonment, and martyrdom. They faced illness with few medical remedies and virtually no pain relief. Perhaps the hymns and songs they sang enabled them to find courage when their own meager powers had reached their limit. Faced with their own first-century congregational limitations and concerns, hymns and songs inspired them to trust that the God who had sustained them in the past would guide them toward the future.

Take a moment to meditatively read these words from Acts. In this narrative, Paul and Silas are arrested and beaten for healing a Philippian slave girl who had been, according to first-century understandings of mental health, possessed by a spirit of divination.

> After [the authorities] had given [Paul and Silas] a severe flogging, they threw them into prison and ordered the jailer to keep them securely. Following these instructions, he put them in the innermost cell and fastened their feet in the stocks. About midnight Paul and Silas were singing hymns to God, and the prisoners were listening to them.
>
> —Acts 16:23–25

Imagine that! Singing and praying behind prison bars! Take a few moments to reflect on your own lifespan: When have you experienced personal tragedy, loss of reputation, or physical or mental suffering? What helped you get through to the other side? Were any hymns or songs pivotal for you in discovering God's presence and maintaining your hope and courage during these challenging times?

When Bruce's mother unexpectedly died from a pulmonary embolism (a blood clot in her lung), he found solace in a hymn sung at her funeral, "It Is Well with My Soul." Later he learned that this hymn was written by Horatio Spofford following the death of his four daughters in the sinking of the *SS Ville du Havre*.

> When peace, like a river, attendeth my way,
> when sorrows like sea billows roll;
> whatever my lot, thou hast taught me to say,
> it is well, it is well with my soul.[3]

Many years later, when his son Matt was diagnosed with a rare form of cancer, Bruce spent much of his morning walk singing two hymns. In the days immediately following the diagnosis, he chanted the *Kyrie*, "Lord, have mercy upon me. Christ, have mercy upon me. Lord, have mercy upon me." As a theologian and preacher, accustomed to the power of words to transform our perceptions of reality, Bruce was reduced to a simple cry for God's help and presence to respond to his feelings of powerlessness. As the days went on and hope returned, Bruce often sang his favorite hymn from his Baptist childhood, "Great Is Thy Faithfulness," which invokes God's enduring love and compassion throughout all the seasons of life.[4]

Today, as Matt and his wife, Ingrid, contemplate starting a family, Bruce knows firsthand that God is faithful and can be counted on in sickness and health, in life and death. He experienced the fidelity of God during these difficult days by embracing the songs of faith he first learned in a small-town church; through the fervent prayers of his congregation and seminary in Lancaster, Pennsylvania, and of people across the world; and through the sustaining power of life-transforming hymns of faith.

Following the unexpected death of his son Chad in 2003, Daryl read the following statement as he introduced a hymn at an Advent concert he was conducting.

> Some of you may know about the recent, tragic death of our son Chad on November 1. It was a sudden blow to our family and friends. Our fast-paced schedule came to a screeching halt. We all faced our grief in different ways. My wife thought a lot about Mary and the pain she must have endured in also losing a son. I looked toward music to help in the healing process. I needed to give a voice to my tears, so I felt compelled to compose. I was looking for a song that matched my emotions. I soon found an Advent carol—"The Angel Gabriel from Heaven Came." The song is about the annunciation, the story of the angel Gabriel coming to Mary. It has a melancholy tune. The opening "Gloria" isn't the full-throated song the angels sang at Christmastime. No, this was Advent. I was waiting for the celebration of the coming of the Messiah. My song was weak and faint, much like the "Gloria" of this song. I'm sure Mary had much apprehension about what was to come. Did she have a sense of the outcome—that her son would bear the sins of the world and endure a horrible death?

The mood of this song seems to reflect the anguish that Mary would experience in losing her son.

One week after Chad's death, I finished this arrangement and put a dedication at the top of the piece. It reads: "To my loving wife, Bonnie, who, like Mary, knows the anguish of losing a son. November 2003."

Like childhood lullabies, the hymns of faith give individuals and communities hope and courage, and inspire us to face our fears amid the darkness that surrounds us. Our personal faith stories reflect the dynamic interplay of worship, music, and theology in the life of faith communities and congregants. For example, the spiritual popularized by gospel singer Ethel Waters proclaims,

> I sing because I'm happy,
> I sing because I'm free,
> for his eye is on the sparrow,
> and I know he's watching me"[5]

We can sing because our songs remind us that God is with us and that nothing, not even our greatest fears, can separate us from God's love.

Our hymns and songs deepen and strengthen our faith as individuals and members of faith communities in life's most difficult times. Bruce regularly teaches a doctoral course at Wesley Theological Seminary in Washington, D.C., on the theme of narrative collapse and restoration. He invites his students to reflect on their experiences of loss, suffering, and tragedy in the context of reading the stories of others who have discovered God's presence as they walked through the darkest valley. He reminds his students to recognize how the loss of one's personal or corporate life story, after pain and struggle, can be the rebirth of a new and life-transforming story.

After a major drop in the stock market, a terrorist attack on our nation, a tornado that destroys the church building, the loss of a job, a case of pastoral misconduct in our congregation, or the diagnosis of a life-threatening illness, we must let go of one image of our lives and world to embrace God's new vision for our future wholeness. Neither we nor our community will ever be the same again, nor do we want to repeat life as it was. But we may discover that by living our faith through the hymns we sing, the community with which we pray, and the beliefs that empower us, we can begin again and again, trusting God's power of new creation. We discover a new song and life story through which we can respond to the trials and celebrations of life.

As most small congregations look at their prospects, they are uncertain about their future and their ability to marshal the spiritual, financial, and corporate resources necessary for long-term survival. Many small congregations yearn for a life-transforming song or story that will enable them to be hopeful, active, and faithful, regardless of what the future brings. Small congregations need to sing songs to face the challenges of life with courage and hope.

SONGS FOR EVERY SEASON OF LIFE

The philosopher Alfred North Whitehead invokes the hymn "Abide with Me" as descriptive of the rhythm of change and changelessness and life and death that characterizes our lives and defines the spiritual quest.[6]

> Abide with me;
> fast falls the eventide.[7]

Night is falling, life is ebbing, and nothing remains the same, not even the beloved traditions of worship in a small congregation. We sit at the bedside, awaiting the final breath, or return from the courthouse, no longer husband and wife. Life is shattered, and we wonder if we can ever go on. This was part of the philosopher Whitehead's own story as well. Although he was raised the son of an Anglican priest, he became an agnostic as an adult. But when he witnessed the loss of a generation of young men, including his own child Eric, on the battlefields of World War I, Whitehead discovered a God who treasures our lives in their entirety. Whitehead came to believe that God is "the fellow sufferer who understands"[8] and the lifelong companion whose tender care embraces and preserves the totality of our lives.

Surely, we live in an ever-changing world where loss is often necessary for growth and progress. Yet a living faith finds its strength in the affirmation that God's faithfulness will stand the test of time. Even if we must let go of all that we hold most dear, whether through the ravages of Alzheimer's disease, terminal illness, or the closing of our church, our lives remain in the everlasting memory of God.

Yes, "fast falls the eventide." Life is a flowing stream, constantly moving into the emerging future. Whether in worship or personal life, the passage of time requires us to let go of "old ways," even ways that served us well in an earlier time. But still we need the "everlasting arms" of God and a fellowship of companions to help us face courageously and creatively the ever-changing nature of life's holy adventure in all its tragic beauty. Our rituals of worship and the hymns and songs we sing awaken us as individuals and communities of faith to the deeper melody of God's ever-sustaining and ever-inspiring presence in our lives.

In times of celebration and loss, we can discover God's presence in the hymns we sing and the presence in worship of faithful companions in the body of Christ. To explore the role that worship and music play in providing hope and healing amid all the seasons of life, we will reflect on songwriter John Ylvisaker's

"I Was There to Hear Your Borning Cry." We will focus on the importance of worship and music in three seasons of life—birth, aging, and death and bereavement—in times of personal and community transition. In meaningful worship, we discover words for our experiences and images that help us face uncertainty, change, and transition. If positive and negative changes alike provoke feelings of anxiety, then congregational worship needs to embrace both celebration and tragedy. A common voice, expressed in a community of lifelong friends, reminds us that we are not alone and that God is our ever-resourceful companion in joy as well as sorrow.

Baptism and Communion as Sources of Hope

Members of small congregations, because of their intimacy, often are able to follow one another's lives through every season from birth to death. John Ylvisaker's words capture the personal and congregational adventure from birth to death and beyond:

> I was there to hear your borning cry,
> I'll be there when you are old.
> I rejoiced the day you were baptized,
> to see your life unfold.[9]

As Bruce writes these words, he remembers last Saturday night's baptism at Disciples United Community Church. Two children from one family, ages three months and nine years, were welcomed into the family of God through the waters of baptism. Life has not been easy for the children's two mothers, but they were committed to raising their children in a community that believes God's grace embraces every kind of family. Marginalized in other communities because of the nature of their holy relationship, they found a home and healing hospitality in our small Saturday-evening church.

While the infant will not consciously remember his baptism, the nine-year-old will always recall the day she stood before our community of thirty congregants and heard that she was God's beloved daughter and that God would be her companion all the days of her life. Our prayer as a community of faith is that these words become life-sustaining affirmations for her whenever she experiences the world as a place of judgment and alienation, that she will always know that her worth is grounded in God's love, and that God's love is everlasting and nonnegotiable, regardless of what the world says about her or how she views herself. As we pray for her, we remember that God's words to Jesus, "you are my beloved," apply to us as well.

Our community's belief in her value as a child of God was confirmed when she was asked to help pass the bread and the cup around the communion circle. For us at Disciples United Community Church, communion truly embodies the real presence of God in the passing of the peace, the affirmation of God's grace through the sacraments of baptism and communion, and the recognition that God's abundant life is ours to experience and share. While we recognize that our congregation is rare in inviting people of all ages to share in God's embodied grace in the sacraments, her participation in serving communion reflects our affirmation that she can be a leader and teacher right now and not only when she has earned the proper credentials or reached an acceptable age.

In small congregations, children matter, not only because of the community's intimacy but also because children's gifts of participation and faith are essential to the community's well-being and vitality in worship. Despite the challenges small congregations face, the welcome of children, and also adults, in baptism is a sign that God is with us, that God loves us, and that God will never abandon us. We are inscribed on the palms of God's hands and forever joined with God, our creator, companion, and savior. This divine promise-keeping applies to communities as well as individuals.

Baptism represents a covenant among God, the one who is baptized, and the community of faith. This is especially true in small congregations for whose members each birth and baptism is a sign of hope and promise. When small congregations are tempted to see the future in terms of limitation rather than growth, and fear rather than hope, baptism affirms that God will be with them, whatever the future holds for their membership, finances, and sustainability.

The intimacy of small congregations calls them to be promise-makers and promise-keepers to those who are baptized: they promise that they will grow along with the child or adult who is baptized. Such promise-keeping isn't always easy for small congregations. But they are called to venture along new pathways, embracing new forms of worship and music, as they share the traditions of faith with children growing up in their community. Worship leaders must listen to, as well as share their faith with, growing children, teenagers, and young adults. Listening well to children and young adults means that we experience their lives, cultural mores, media, and music through their youthful eyes rather than those of judgment or traditions that are meaningful to us but outmoded to them. It means receiving their gifts and exploring their youthful "traditions" as well as witnessing to our traditions of faith and worship.

In small churches, children can be leaders right now; they can sing in the choir, hand out bulletins, read Scripture, share reflections, and even celebrate communion. Young adults and mature teens and preteens can even participate in worship planning.

A recently confirmed high-school student commented after several months of service on the worship committee:

> At first, I didn't have much to say, and the meetings were boring, just talking about flower arrangements and old hymns. But when they turned to me and asked what I needed to experience God at church, and when they listened to what I had

to say, I felt I belonged, and it wasn't just old people's church anymore. And, to my surprise, they are including some of my ideas in the Sunday service. While I still sleep in and miss church once in a while, especially after a party or game on Saturday night, I look forward to church now, and I'm glad that I can make a difference here. I even invite my friends to come, when they're sleeping over on Saturday nights.

A healthy and vital small congregation commits itself to grow along with its youth, to experiment with new forms of media and worship, and to let go of outworn traditions and embrace novel ways of worship that reflect and nurture the faith of children and young adults. This applies to people of all ages. As one senior adult noted:

> I never thought that I would be playing a drum in *this* church, but when my I see my six-year-old grandson joyfully playing beside me, I know that this is what it means to be church for him, and now this is church for me too! I'm so happy when I hear his mom report that he wakes up early on Sunday mornings, eager to go to church!

Truly, the liturgy is the people's work, and people of all ages can play important roles in worship in small congregations.

The interplay of baptism and communion in the ongoing life of a small congregation reminds us that God's everlasting grace calls us into life, inspires the formation and growth of faith communities, and provides the resources we need to be faithful as communities in every season of life. Regularly sharing in the celebration of communion, we discover with the Caribbean hymn that "loaves abound,"[10] that great things emerge from small beginnings, and that God's grace is sufficient for us regardless of our current budget or membership. Aware of God's unconditional and ever-creative grace, we affirm God's inspiring presence in everyone who joins us for worship.

Aging, Death, and Hope

In small congregations, what is individual is also communal. The well-being of the community and the people is bound together most especially when communities experience grief and loss due to death and aging. An ancient church father noted that Jesus lived through all the seasons of life from birth to death so that every season of life would become an opportunity for humans to experience holiness and to share in Jesus's life, death, and resurrection. While this church father no doubt addressed his spiritual counsel to individuals, this same wisdom applies to the seasons of congregational life, where the deaths of individuals can shake a congregation's faith in its own survival. As a result of their size, small congregations have fewer buffers than larger ones against the realities of infirmity, diminishment, and death. Everyone matters in the life of small congregations. As the *United Church of Christ Book of Worship* asserts, "In the Christian community, death is a corporate experience that touches the life of the entire family of faith."[11] At such moments, friends, family members, and congregations need to embrace personal and corporate grief and loss in light of God's faithful companionship.

Members of small congregations experience firsthand Paul's vision of the interdependent body of Christ: "When one member suffers, all suffer together with it; when one member is honored, all rejoice together with it" (1 Cor. 12:26). Like individuals whose health depends on a delicate and intricate balance of many factors, the well-being of small congregations depends on the well-being of every part. Each member has a place and a role, and although these roles can be confining in backward-looking congregations, they are often life-giving for both the member herself or himself and the congregation.

When the board chairman of a seventy-five-member United Church of Christ congregation died unexpectedly of a heart attack, more than a few members of the board wondered aloud,

"How will we get along without Steve? He was the heart and soul of this church." When an aging couple who had printed the bulletins and served as greeters for more than thirty years in an urban church became unable to perform their functions, there were whispers among the fifty active members: "How can we help them let go of these duties? But who will take their place?" When the eighty-seven-year-old volunteer organist of a fifty-member rural United Methodist church began to lose her sight and struggled to play for Sunday worship—a task she had faithfully performed since age sixteen—the part-time pastor and the worship committee wondered how they could most gracefully respond to the diminishing quality of her work. They also asked whether they could find a new organist and, if so, how they would be able to pay a professional musician.

For both individuals and congregations, change always means loss and the challenge to adapt to new realities in our individual and corporate lives. The question for small congregations is this: Will they creatively choose their destiny and vocation for this time and place in their history, whether this means joyfully embracing their diminished membership, taking new initiatives, or merging with another congregation? Psychologist Victor Frankl, in writing of his experiences as a Jewish prisoner in a Nazi concentration camp, asserts: "Everything can be taken away from a man but one thing—the last of human freedoms—to choose one's attitude in any given set of circumstances."[12] Congregations, like individuals, always have the choice to embrace life right where they are and to live joyfully, regardless of demographic or economic challenges.

Aging is, as John Ylvisaker's hymn notes, part of life's unfolding for individuals and congregations. Life-affirming worship embraces aging, noting that "for everything there is a season" (Eccles. 3:1). Healthy communal and personal spirituality involves embracing, personally and corporately, the season of life in which we find ourselves, and discovering God's presence even in aging and diminishment. Small, aging congregations have many gifts—the gifts of intimacy, tradition, and history—that need to be affirmed and celebrated. They also have the gift of faithful endurance. All these gifts can be inspiring and enlivening to others and can be nurtured by creative worship. In the spirit of Anna and Simeon in the Jerusalem Temple, who alone recognized the baby Jesus as God's chosen one, small and aging congregations can experience and share God's surprising and rejuvenating presence through exploring new possibilities in congregational worship, even as they proclaim their faith through familiar melodies.

When small congregations live in a spirit of abundance rather than scarcity, they can become communities of vitality and inspiration, regardless of what the future portends. Listen to the witness of small congregations in difficult settings that have chosen to live in terms of God's abundant life. An eighty-year-old choir member from a small Presbyterian church noted:

> Yes, we're small, and we'll probably not grow much since our town is losing population. But we decided to do something new, and it's changed this church: we started a small food pantry for the growing number of unemployed people in our county. We've also decided to buy the new hymnbook to place alongside the hymnbook from the mid-fifties. We still like the old hymns, but some of the new global hymns have really livened up worship! Some of the old-timers are even clapping their hands!

Faced with diminishing membership and few prospects of growth, a small United Church of Christ congregation in Eastern Pennsylvania decided to replace the pews with portable chairs after voting to "nest" a new church start in the building. A lay leader explained:

> We realized that given who we were as a congregation, and all the data on church growth, our congregation would most likely continue to decline numerically regardless of what

initiatives we might take. So we made a decision to work with the denomination to provide a place for a newly started congregation aiming at young adults to meet. We were grief-stricken, at first, when we pondered our own death as a congregation. But, then we remembered the message of Easter. Even if we die as a congregation, we can give life to a new and vital congregation.

Rather than sitting on its financial assets, this congregation invested in the future by remodeling the sanctuary and buying new hymnals, appropriate to a younger congregation as well as to its own worship needs. While the two congregations will worship separately most Sundays, they plan to meet together quarterly and for special services on holiday weekends. They also plan to gather regularly for social events and educational opportunities. The older congregation will provide the gifts of tradition and a space for worship, while the younger congregation will bring novelty and diversity to the joint services.

In reflecting on the brevity of life, the wisdom teacher of Ecclesiastes notes that there is "a time to be born and a time to die" (Eccles. 3:2). This is true for congregations as well as individuals. Over the years, Bruce has read a number of histories of small United Church of Christ congregations in Pennsylvania. Most were founded with the dream of sharing the gospel and training children of rural communities to live by the faith of their parents and grandparents. Their histories tell the story of generosity and sacrifice, of challenge and faithfulness. Many congregations born two hundred years ago with vision and promise are now barely surviving; some have always been small but wonder about their viability a decade from now as young adults leave the farm and small-town life. Death is a real possibility for small congregations in rural and urban areas. As they look at diminishing memberships and fragile futures in light of lively memories of baptisms, wedding celebrations, youth and young couples groups, and vibrant music programs, many congregations are dominated by feelings of grief and loss. Many wonder if their best days are behind them and if they still have a vocation in their communities.

As we noted earlier, death hangs especially heavy in small congregations. Death often means the loss of an intimate friend or a colleague in the choir or men's group. It may even be the tipping point toward congregational death. Just as families live through the grief of the empty place at the table, congregations live through the empty pew and the missing voice. The deaths of faithful members remind small congregations of their own fragility. At such times, worship grounds us in the realities of grief and loss but also provides a sense of God's faithfulness through every season of life. Theologically grounded worship, practiced over time in communities of faith, shapes our character and our response to tragedy. It also provides a sense of continuity and trustworthiness that enables us to face the necessary losses of personal and congregational life with hope and endurance. As the United Church of Christ Service of "Thanksgiving for One Who Has Died" proclaims: "Friends, we gather here in the protective shelter of God's healing love. We are free to pour out our grief, release our anger, face our emptiness, and know that God cares. . . . For whether we live or die, we belong to Christ who is Lord both of the dead and of the living."[13]

In the songs we sing, the Scriptures we read, and the testimonies we give, we affirm that each life matters to our community and to God, and that each person—and each faith community—finds its ultimate fulfillment through God's everlasting love. Reminded of our own mortality as individuals and communities of faith, we can still sing "Alleluia" and live gracefully in the spirit of Dag Hammarskjold's prayer:

> For all that has been—Thanks.
> For all that shall be—Yes.[14]

Even when a small congregation chooses to conclude its visible ministry, its impact goes on in those whose lives have been transformed in worship, church-school classes, mission and outreach, and pastoral care. Bruce remembers the final service at Bethesda Christian Church (Disciples of Christ) in Bethesda, Maryland. Unable to marshal the finances or sustain the corporate energy to operate a large church building, the church voted to sell its building and contribute the proceeds to support new church starts and regional congregational vitality programs. Following its final celebration of communion, the congregation and friends sang an old familiar hymn, "Living for Jesus," as a reminder that "nothing can separate us from the love of God in Christ Jesus our Lord." Though the building would soon close, worshipers experienced resurrection in imagining future congregations that would emerge as a result of their fidelity.

> Living for Jesus a life that is true,
> striving to please him in all that I do;
> yielding allegiance, glad-hearted and free,
> this is the pathway of blessing for me.
> O Jesus, Lord and Savior, I give myself to thee,
> for thou, in thy atonement, didst give thyself for me;
> I own no other master, my heart shall be thy throne,
> my life I give, henceforth to live, O Christ, for thee alone.[15]

Worship in small congregations can be challenging, but as we've proclaimed throughout this book, it can also be beautiful as the members faithfully live out their vocations as the body of Christ through meaningful service and worship. Small congregations can be places of faithful transformation and reassurance when they honestly face their limitations and provide comfort in times of national upheaval. The songs we sing and the faith we affirm in a gathered community year after year give us hope and courage to face gracefully and courageously all the seasons of life, knowing that in life and death, God is our loving companion.

ENLIVENING WORSHIP AND MUSIC IN THE SMALL CHURCH

To make the words of this chapter come alive for you, we invite you to reflect on the hymns, songs, and Scriptures that have sustained you during times of transition, grief, loss, and change. In your memory, go back to a period of significant change in your life. What Scriptures or devotional readings gave you courage and inspiration? What hymns or songs deepened your faith and inspired you to face life's challenges and changes?

Reflect on the hymns, songs, and Scriptures you've heard at loved ones' funeral services.

+ Which ones were most meaningful to you? How did they sustain you?
+ As you look toward the future and your own mortality, what hymns or songs would you like played or sung at your funeral or memorial service?
+ What Scriptures reflect your faith as you consider your own mortality?
+ Where do you find your hope in challenging personal and congregational times?

CHAPTER 10

A TALE OF TWO CHURCHES

SMALL CHURCHES WITH GREAT WORSHIP

IN THIS FINAL CHAPTER, we will share a few images of enlivening worship and music in the small church from the perspective of the congregations we serve as minister of music and co-pastor. St. Peter's United Church of Christ in Lancaster, Pennsylvania, averages sixty in Sunday-morning worship. Disciples United Community Church, two miles west of St. Peter's, fondly known as DUCC or "Duck," averages around thirty-five each Saturday evening. But both churches are alive in worship and mission. Founded in 1906, St. Peter's UCC affirms that it is "shining for a second century" and notes that "we might be over a hundred years old, but new things are happening!" Founded in 2001, DUCC describes itself as a "new seed of hope where there are no strangers" and as "a progressive, inclusive Christian congregation, building a community that spreads Christ's message of God's abundant love for all creation."

Much to our surprise, we discovered that both of these churches held their first worship services at Lancaster Theological Seminary, where we serve on the faculty. In the past few years, both congregations have experienced numerical, spiritual, and missional growth as a result of their commitments to enlivening worship and music. In worship and mission, both congregations think globally and act locally in sharing God's hospitality with refugees and marginalized people. The two of us share our stories as a way of inspiring your own congregation's unique way of enlivening its worship and music.

ST. PETER'S UNITED CHURCH OF CHRIST

An observer entering the sanctuary at St. Peter's would first notice the beautiful stained-glass windows, which portray twelve rather austere males. On a bright day, one might catch the sunlight casting a holy aura throughout the space. The windows portray the mystery of God as the multifaceted designs display powerful biblical stories. In keeping with the church's reformed roots, Zwingli and Luther are positioned among several apostles and prophets set within magnificent stone arches. This neo-Gothic structure has high ceilings, a large reredos with deep burgundy drapes, and lovely wooden pews facing the large rose window above the high altar. Visitors might think they have stepped back in time. What relevance can this traditional-looking church have to its twenty-first-century neighborhood? How can worship speak to a multicultural, interfaith neighborhood in a place such as this? Is it possible to honor the architecture of this treasure and its traditions and still worship in a way that is enriching and that changes lives?

Pastor Bonnie Hollinger and its members answer with a hearty "Absolutely!" The worship at St. Peter's is eclectic and yet in many ways traditional. In the past three years, nurtured by the vision of the pastor, the congregation embarked on a capital campaign to enrich the lovely space and make it more hospitable. The members chose an architect who was willing to preserve the windows, the wood, and the holy space, and yet design a narthex that would be used primarily for holding coffee time, greeting visitors, and assisting the homeless who often come on Sunday mornings for help. The architectural changes are in keeping with this small congregation's desire to revere its traditions and yet worship in a way that allows for an outpouring of gifts in word, music, sacrament, and hospitality.

When looking at the Sunday bulletin, an observer would see a fairly traditional order of service. The pastor and Daryl—the minister of music and the pastor's husband—have kept the basic order of the service that has been practiced for years but have transformed the service through global music, drama, media, additional musical instruments, dance, visual art, altar adornments, and interactive liturgy. A key to successfully implementing change and strengthening worship has been the generous spirit of the congregation and the co-leadership of the pastor and minister of music.

Worship at St. Peter's is truly eclectic, and living out a cohesive service can be tricky if one does not always stay attuned to the theology and purpose of worship. Richard Berg, a UCC pastor who serves as the director of the Lancaster Seminary Library, commented, "Everything centers on the Scriptures from the time I walk in the door until I leave. The lesson is driven home in multiple ways. We sing it, we read it, and we hear it preached." At St. Peter's, the service embodies our belief that Scripture is made flesh through its connection to all of life, both in worship and in our daily lives. This approach to worship does not happen haphazardly. When Pastor Bonnie and Daryl meet to plan worship, they begin with the lectionary for the day. While this is not a practice for all congregations, following the Christian calendar fits well with the theology of this congregation as it seeks to join tradition and novelty in worship for the service of God. They look at the texts and decide which passage will be central for the day. This attention to the Christian seasons enables them to craft a service that reflects their commitment to growing through the Scriptures, listening to God, and maintaining a strong commitment to their neighbors and each other.

St. Peter's worship space awakens people to the holy and is adorned to engage the worshiper with a sense of God's presence. The altar, the windows, the communion table, and even the narthex and bulletin invite worshipers to encounter the mystery and wonder of God.

A parishioner recalls a time during Lent when she experienced the cross in a way unlike ever before. The altar had been stripped, and no flowers were present in the sanctuary. Bare, stark tree branches were placed on the altar, draped with black cloth. A dozen or so crosses of varying sizes and shapes were positioned in the chancel area. The bulletin explained that the altar was prepared this way to guide the worshipers in a Lenten time of fasting and discipline. Other art forms helped reinforce the theme for the day. During the confession, Pastor Bonnie danced to music that Daryl improvised on the organ. She lifted up objects that often lure us away from God—a large wad of money, a gaudy purse, even a beautiful gold cross necklace. She danced with joy as she embraced all these objects. As she drew nearer to the crosses, her dance indicated her internal conflict. She portrayed the struggle of giving up things to carry one of the ugly wooden crosses. No words were spoken, but through music, dance, and the altar presentation, the need to confess was clear. Some members found themselves in tears as they were nudged to worship God anew. "I found myself identifying with the struggle of consumerism and not wanting to go the way of the cross of Jesus. I much preferred the pretty cross than the way in which Jesus asks us to deny ourselves and follow him," one person commented.

Dance and altar adornment work well in the sanctuary at St. Peter's. The space also accommodates various forms of electronic technology. We have taken care to position the screen on which we project our PowerPoint presentations so as not to distract from the beauty of the sanctuary. During renovations, we discovered a surface where a board displaying hymn numbers had been hung. Since we use bulletins, this was no longer needed. We left the space blank, and it is perfect for projections. We do not have to deal with large screens blocking our beautiful altar or setting up and taking down equipment, and yet everyone can see the images.

We combined music and projected art in a powerful way during a time of confession. Daryl taught the congregation a simple *Kyrie* that he composed and that was easily learned by rote. As we sang it, Bonnie portrayed images of our broken world—including hungry children, homeless families, refugees, people with addictions, photos of our own congregation, and empty pews. While we meditated on these, we sang the *Kyrie* over and over. This ritual gave the community the opportunity for both personal and corporate confessions of our sins of commission and omission. We used the Scripture "As you have done it to the least of these, you do it unto me" (Matt. 25:40) as our focus for the day. A member remarked that she was able to discover through this simple yet powerful part of our worship ways in which she is part of the larger kingdom of God and how her life affects others. We believe that when folk can engage in, rather than merely observe worship, greater is the praise to God and the commitment to each other and the community in which we live.

When any of us enters church, it is sometimes difficult to prepare for worship. We often come to worship distracted by the joys and burdens of the week, church business, the messages in the worship bulletin and other handouts, and the chatter of greeting one another. We believe that our worship together is a holy place and time. One of the ways we motivate folk to prepare for a rich dialogue with God and others is to set aside a time of preparation. A processional during Advent is an example of a powerful and amazing call to worship. A cantor came into the sanctuary singing "Waiting for Your Presence."

Daryl Hollinger

Wait - ing, wait - ing,   wait-ing for your pre - sence.

Wait - ing,   wait - ing,   come in - car - nate One.

As she reached the chancel rail, she turned around and invited the congregation to join in both the motions and the song. The song began with people opening their palms, which helped us release the tensions we carried and also open our hearts and hands to what God had in store for us. This gesture reinforced the theology of the incarnation of God in our lives. The simplicity of the song and motions allowed those present to participate without looking at a bulletin. We believe this ritual was implanted within our hearts for the week as a mantra for living in the Advent season amid the frantic holiday time of the secular world.

At St. Peter's, music is just as central to worship as the liturgy is. Sometimes we discover that the music shapes the entire service. We have discussed in previous chapters how music is chosen, how it bears our theology, how it needs to be accessible, how we note its historical context—and all of this is exposed again as we prepare the service. It is the firm belief of the congregation that the minister of music is a co-minister in the life of our parish. This is borne out in the way we unlock the talents of many folk who thought they could never "do music."

To look at our choir, one might conclude that it is a traditional group. We sit in the chancel, wear robes, practice once a week, and typically sing an anthem. That is perhaps where the "traditional" part ends. Our primary purpose is to lead the people's song. It is true that we traditionally prepare an anthem based on the theme of the day and accentuating the Gospel or the Hebrew Scripture. In addition, the choir teaches new songs and hymns and assists in confessionals, singing psalms, leading prayers, interpreting Scriptures, and giving the benediction. Our choir is busy throughout the service, because its members are full leaders and definitely not entertainers. They enliven the assembly song by adding descants, singing in parts, and playing musical instruments. Even some choir members beyond the age of eighty have embraced the drums and improvise on hymns. One elderly woman recently said, "I have always dreamed of playing the drums, and now I am doing it."

Gifts are being discovered because we are open to serving God in many ways. Daryl has introduced hand chimes, handbells, and other percussion instruments to many parts of the liturgy, and people readily volunteer to play them. We see the whole process from choir practice to worship as an act of prayer, and offer these gifts as part of our love for God and each other. We believe that even though we are small, we can have great music. During choir rehearsals, we take time to discuss the theology of the music and the mission we live through it. Our fourteen choir members fully believe that they play an important part not only in our worship but also in helping shape our faith and living it daily.

We are especially thrilled to have such high-quality music in a small congregation. We believe that God takes even the smallest gift and enlarges it. We assert that music is transformative. One of our members, Shirley, tells how a song compelled her decision to serve our parish in a new and exciting way. She recalls Pastor Bonnie asking her if she would be willing to serve as consistory, or board, president. Although Shirley had served in many areas of the church, she said she did not feel capable. "I don't think I'm good enough to do it," she said. Daryl had chosen the third verse of "Take My Gifts" by Shirley Erena Murray for us to sing as we brought our offerings to the altar. We sang it for a whole season to the tune HOLY MANNA in a full-throated, early American style. There was no holding back in the singing. It demanded the worshiper's full participation. Shirley continued, "Every week we sang, 'Take whatever I can offer, gifts that I have yet to find.' As I sang that, I realized that God was calling me to do the job on consistory. That song helped me discover what I needed to do to serve." Shirley has reminded us of God's call in her life many times when we have wavered in our faith to grow our church. It is a powerful testimony to the transformative nature of music and how, when shared, it can profoundly lead us all.

This testimony is borne out especially in our call to let our light shine in our neighborhood, which has led us to open our doors to folk from many other cultures. On some Sundays we might look like a typical Caucasian Protestant group of worshipers. However, part of our mission has been to embrace the refugees who are settling in our neighborhood. When we saw the need for jobs, transportation, and English instruction, we knew that God was calling us to be good neighbors. It is in serving others that we embrace other cultures. In reaching out to our neighbors, we have embraced their music and language in our worship. Currently, four congregations meet at St. Peter's: Church of the Fraternity (Haitian), Lancaster Chin Christian Fellowship (Burmese), La Senda Antiqua (Hispanic), and St. Peter's United Church of Christ (Ethiopian, Native American, and Caucasian).

To help us assimilate to these new cultures, we are introducing music in our own worship services that propels us to share the love of God in new and exciting ways. Daryl has taught the congregation and the choir many global songs. It is not surprising to find us singing a gathering song from Brazil, a prayer chant from Pakistan, or a sending song from Cameroon. One of the great blessings of the folks at St. Peter's is their willingness to try almost anything. We do this with great reverence and appreciation for the gifts of song from other cultures.

All of this has prepared us for the joint services we sometimes share. One Christmas Eve, we worshiped with the Haitian and Burmese congregations as well as with Bhutanese refugees new to the United States. The Christmas story and parts of the liturgy were presented in each native tongue. The holy family was portrayed by Burmese teenagers from the surrounding neighborhood. Each group offered its gifts by bringing its unique ethnic and liturgical style to the service, a celebration of the Nativity though drama, dance, and music. Our Hindu neighbors also came to celebrate with us. They said, "There is one God, and we will dance to your little baby Jesus." How rich and encompassing this experience was as we truly lived our faith in loving God with all our hearts, and our neighbor as ourselves (Matt. 22:37–39). As we celebrated the Holy Feast, everyone was invited to participate, in keeping with our belief that all people are welcome at God's table.

Even though we are a small congregation, that night our sanctuary was full, and it was truly a neighborhood celebration as well as a gathering of the many cultures that meet at St. Peter's. We have been preparing for such a time as this by singing global music, allowing ourselves to be flexible in worship, and refusing to believe that being small inhibits our ability to let our lights shine for God.

Henri Nouwen, noted Catholic spirituality writer, once said, "The great news of the gospel is precisely that God became small and vulnerable and hence bore fruit among us."[1] In this spirit, we open ourselves to God and allow God to use us even though we are small. When people hear of all the work that is being done in our parish, they often comment that we must be a large congregation. We reply, "We are small, but God is faithful."

DISCIPLES UNITED COMMUNITY CHURCH

Throughout this book, we have affirmed that small and struggling congregations can be places of lively and inspiring worship and music for every season of life.[2] Behind the humble and often nondescript exteriors of small churches, each week lives are transformed and people are called to be God's partners in healing the world.

If you looked at the facade of the Friends Meeting House in Lancaster, Pennsylvania, at 4:00 P.M. on a Saturday afternoon, you wouldn't anticipate the spiritually lively evening to come. The building is simple, and the community room where Disciples United Community Church worships is plain and utilitarian. But within an hour, you would experience a small but dedicated community, worshiping, sharing ideas, wrestling with new theological concepts, and exploring what it means to follow Jesus in outreach and mission. DUCC is a small congregation that joins lively worship with solid progressive Christian theology.[3]

A typical gathering begins at 4:30 P.M. on a warm Saturday afternoon, when a handful of automobiles pull into the parking lot. Laden with boxes of fabric, banners, freshly baked bread, and snacks, DUCC members begin their weekly task of joyfully creating a cathedral of spirit from a nondescript community room. As greetings are exchanged and hugs given, the small team that will lead worship begins to assemble, shape, and adorn the worship space. Folding chairs form an elongated circle, with a simple music stand serving as a pulpit at one end and a round communion table in the center. At times, the presenters of the week's "reflections" place a chair in front of the pulpit for a more dialogical style of preaching or to facilitate *lectio divina*, or "holy reading," with the congregation. Soon, banners and fabric from around the world adorn the space. Each week, dynamic order emerges from chaos; beauty bursts forth from functionality; sacredness arises from the ordinary.

Like Jacob awakening from his dream of a ladder of angels, the community room comes alive with beauty as we discover, in the spirit of Jacob's exclamation, that in this simple and ordinary space, "God is here and we know it." Diane Pyles, who serves as assistant minister for liturgy and arts, affirms:

Preparing the space is an act of homemaking with hospitality as the main priority. Crossing the threshold from the parking lot to our worship space awakens us to the presence of the Holy. Our creative adorning of the worship space provides endless possibilities for enhancing the message birthed from the biblical text. Each week, our worship place is different as we add a splash of color and invite our community and strangers to experience a sense of mystery and surprise.

The dynamic call and response between Word and Table characterizes our worship space. Worship flows from Word to Table, and back again. We are people who believe that God is still speaking in our chants; hymns; prayers of praise, thanksgiving, and supplication; healing touch; and weekly communion. But we equally affirm that our worship reflects divine inspiration embodied in theological reflections, in healing hugs, in the people gathered around the communion table, and in sung words of many cultures and languages. It is here in worship that hospitality is best practiced. In the spirit of Isaiah's mystical experience in the temple (Isa. 6:1–8), our worship aims to awaken all of our senses, so that we may proclaim in awe and gratitude that "the whole earth is full of God's glory."

At DUCC, the clutter and chaos of our lives, like the rearranged community room where we worship, are transformed into materials for worship and beauty of experience. Divine artistry is seen in the building up and the breaking down of our "sacred space" that characterize the journeys of our worship and congregation. Each Saturday, our own artistry in creating a holy space reflects God's artistry in inspiring creativity in each moment of experience.

As we approach 4:45 P.M., the atmosphere gradually changes in the community room. Seamlessly we join the sacred space of worship with the sacred time of study, which is also a form of worship. In another circle in the community room, fifteen to twenty of the thirty-five regular participants gather for study. At DUCC, we affirm that we are called to love God with our mind as well as heart and hands. Whole-person experiential faith embraces mind, body, spirit, and relationships in a dynamic and ever-creative interplay. Theological education is imaginative as well as intellectual as we explore new ways to interpret and experience our relationship with God and God's mission for us as followers of Jesus.

As each study hour begins with a time of silent meditation, breath prayer, or centering prayer, the final aesthetic touches of the worship space are completed by the worship team. At DUCC, we have learned to practice the art of spiritual multitasking as we prepare for worship and still our hearts for study, listen for the laughter and wisdom of our children who play on the rug at the outside edge of the worship circle, chant as we move in procession to the communion table, and sing the hymns of many lands. We have discovered that we can "practice the presence of God" in every aspect of worship: whether we are setting up chairs, greeting a visitor, participating in a class, sharing our reflections on Scripture, or giving or receiving communion.

Unabashedly progressive and open and affirming of the experiences and insights of the GLBTQ[4] community, the gifts of science, and the wisdom of global spiritualities, we gather to transform our minds through meditation, *lectio divina*, imaginative prayer, and body prayer. These are the prelude to serious theological reflection on topics such as process theology and spiritual formation; hard choices in ethics and science; progressive theology; the problem of evil; Jesus in the twenty-first century; healing and wholeness; feminist theology; and the parables of Jesus. Indeed, people often come to DUCC for the first time through study and then stay for lively, interactive, global worship.

Our aim in the study hour is to embody and apply what we study. We have come to church to grow in wisdom and stature, and theological reflection frames our time together. We are here to co-create with God and with one another as new ideas flow from leaders to participants and back again. At DUCC, we are all teachers and learners, seekers and believers, no matter where we are on the journey of life.

Around 5:50 P.M., the movement once again gently shifts from study to worship. At the edge of the circle is the children's space—a colorful quilt with toys, books, crayons, and paper easily available. Intergenerational in spirit, the configuration of worship space allows children to move easily from the children's meditation—what we call "stories for the community"— to play and prayer, or to sitting with their parents. Often the children play percussion instruments, respond to the litanies, and dance with us to the open communion table, eager to share in the bread and juice of divine hospitality. Worship begins with silence and the lighting of the peace candle, followed by the interplay of Scripture, global chants, and traditional and contemporary hymns, as well as times of silence for contemplation interspersed throughout. As we light the candle of peace and global awareness, we remember our interconnectedness with Sudan and Iraq, with their starving children, violence in the streets, and wounded and traumatized soldiers and civilians. On any given Saturday evening, the community sings music from many continents, often accompanied by keyboard, tambourines, castanets, maracas, and other percussive instruments, as well as a cappella. We believe that it is important to hear God's voice in our own voices, whether in English, Lakota, Spanish, or African languages. In an interdependent universe, there is no "us-them" dualism. Our spiritual center is connected with every other spiritual center, and the goal of our worship is to be conscious of the world's many voices without losing our own unique voice.

Singing at DUCC is not a performance, but an opening to Christ's presence in the gathered community. "Singing creates community and is a spiritual practice, inviting people to experience God's voice in our voice, and God's breathing in our breathing," says Diane Pyles. In sharing God's praise, we create experiences of beauty that emerge from the blending of the many and the one.

At DUCC, worship is intended to be highly participatory, and this applies to the reflections on Scripture as well. Prayer bells often invite us to silent reflection after each Scripture reading. At times, our community sermon rises out of an experience of *lectio divina*, in which each person, including children, is asked to reflect prayerfully upon the words of Scripture and then to share her or his insights. At other times, after the sermon, participants are invited to respond to the sermon's theme with the phrase "God is still speaking," and then enter into a time of community dialogue and sharing that enables the words of Scripture and sermon to take new life in the words of the community.

Prayer is equally participatory. After an introductory moment of silence or chant and prayer of thanksgiving by one of the leaders, we enter another time of silence, followed by freely spoken prayers of personal or communal gratitude and intercession. Each spoken prayer is followed by the words "God in all things," to which the worshipers respond "All things in God." Children often join in, sharing their own gratitude and concern for a loved one who is sick or a cousin serving in the military. To the surprise of those who see progressive theology and worship as primarily intellectual, our hymns and prayers are often followed by heartfelt and exuberant "amens" and "hallelujahs."

On the first Saturday of the month, the community continues its time of prayer with a healing circle. Those who wish may come forward for the laying on of hands—for themselves or as a channel for someone for whom they seek healing. Those who remain in their seats are invited to hold an intention for healing for those who come forward. Each week, we seek to be a healing congregation, welcoming and affirming diversity in all its forms, practicing healthy touch, and celebrating God's grace and reconciling love in the eucharistic feast.[5]

At DUCC, our approach to liturgical healing is grounded in our trust that God is working gently and persistently through and in us to bring reconciliation, physical well-being, and emotional wholeness in every situation. Our worship, therefore, is laden with affirmations of God's presence and care. We believe wholeheartedly that God wants us to have abundant life. Accordingly, we believe that God's healing energy is present in the anointing and the laying on of hands, in reiki healing touch, prescription drugs, and surgical procedures.[6] Indeed, all worship is aimed at awakening us to God's healing and inspiring presence in the varied encounters of life.

Holy Communion once again calls our community to movement and participation as the community follows the children who bring gifts of the offering and bread and cup to the table, sometimes dancing but always singing. The table prayers involve words of welcome to all people; pastoral and lay prayers of thanksgiving; and spontaneous gestures of gratitude that include not only passing the peace, but also passing the bread and cup to one another. Sometimes we include body prayers (raising hands, bowing, placing hands together, taking a step forward, or even skipping) in recognition of the graceful action of God's extravagant hospitality embodied in our community's worship. We feed one another in communion, sharing the bread and the cup as a reminder of our community's solidarity within the complex and many-faceted, yet always interdependent, body of Christ, nested within God's abundant yet broken creation. At DUCC, communion is the feast of radical hospitality for all who are present, regardless of age, denomination, sexual orientation, ethnicity, and theological perspective. Holy Communion embodies the spirit of what we describe as "ancient-future-now" worship that joins traditional words and motions with twenty-first-century cosmology and generous and novel descriptions of God's nature and presence through song and liturgy.

Our emerging worship service concludes with the community's turning from the communion table to the door for the "sending forth" blessing. This act embodies our commitment to join our worship with our everyday life, to bring the subversive hospitality of worship to our daily lives and tables, and to go forth awakened to God's glorious realm of hope, love, peace, and shalom.

The feasting continues as what remains of our communion bread becomes the centerpiece of the fellowship time, and our table is extended to include a variety of healthy and, at times, richly caloric refreshments brought in a serendipitous fashion by all who feel so moved. The feasting reminds us that our worship illumines the whole world. Breaking bread around the table awakens us to the holiness of all creation and humankind, including those who suffer from poverty, injustice, and malnutrition.

This eucharistic experience of "lived omnipresence," the recognition that in worship we can truly experience God in the here and now, continues as the novelty of worship and fellowship moves into the novelty of deconstruction, of taking down the banners and adornments and chairs until we meet again. As Diane Pyles notes, "Our worship planning group strives to create worship times that are incarnational and transformational." In the transformation of the worship space, we discover holiness in the plain community room that we will once again beautify with fabrics and prayers when the community gathers next Saturday evening.

THE ADVENTURE CONTINUES

We began our reflections on enlivening worship and music in the small church with the affirmation that although worship in small churches can be challenging, it can also be beautiful. In the course of this book, we have sought to present a holistic vision of worship for small congregations that joins theory and practice, mind and heart, and tradition and innovation. We believe, in the spirit of Jesus's words, that whenever a handful of Christians gather for prayer, Scripture, reflection, and song, Christ is present, inviting us through our worship to a deeper relationship with God and our neighbor.

Small churches face many challenges in creating lively and meaningful worship services. We have experienced these challenges at St. Peter's UCC and Disciples United Community Church. Within the limitations that small congregations face, we believe that God has planted possibilities for spiritual transformation. When small congregations begin to imagine new forms of worship, they will open the door to greater manifestations of divine creativity and human inventiveness.

Small churches have always shared God's light in the world, and we believe that through the interplay of divine call and human response, your congregation's light can shine more brightly in worship and be a blessing to your church and the community where you live. May God bless your congregation on this holy adventure!

WAITING

THREE DRAMAS FOR ADVENT

BY BONNIE HOLLINGER

I. GET OUT OF MY WAY

[Two people sit in chairs—a woman and her teenage child next to each other. The mom mimes driving a car.]

MOTHER: What's with this traffic? We are barely moving. *[Looks at watch.]* We need to be at the youth center in fifteen minutes, and then I have to get to the library to meet my study group. *[exasperated]* I knew we should have left earlier!

YOUTH: It's OK, Mom, I don't mind being a little late. We're just shooting some basketballs. It's not an actual game, you know. We're just practicing and having fun.

MOTHER: *[exasperated]* Lucky for you, but I have a lot to get done! Do you realize that after study group I have to pick you up, then go to the grocery store, get to the bank before it closes, and then we're having your aunt and uncle over for dinner?

YOUTH: All right! I love Aunt Marcy and Uncle Rick. Uncle Rick is always so funny with his stories.

MOTHER: Well, I'm glad somebody thinks he's funny! *[Blares the horn.]* Come on, get moving!

YOUTH: Mom, can't you see we're not going anywhere? There are flashing lights up there. Probably an accident or something. Why don't you just take a chill pill? You're always getting on me about being hyper.

MOTHER: *[glares at youth.]* A lot you know about waiting! Do you know how much time I spend waiting? I wait in lines at the grocery store, the bank, the post office. I even had to wait at the dry cleaner yesterday. I just want to hurry up and get going.

YOUTH: *[shrugs shoulders]* OK, Mom, but I'm going to chill, if you know what I mean. Listen to my tunes! *[Puts headset on and listens to iPod.]*

MOTHER: *[throws hands up in disgust and reaches for a book]* Well, I might as well study if I have to sit here. No sense letting all this time go to waste!

YOUTH: What-EV-er!

II. I JUST GOTTA HAVE IT NOW!

[A couple are in conversation at the dinner table.]

PARTNER 1: You know, honey, I think I finally found the solution to our dilemma about our Christmas gift for my mother this year. She's always so hard to buy for, and every year we just keep changing our minds about what to get.

PARTNER 2: You are right about that. She has everything she needs. Maybe we should give her some money. But what's your solution?

PARTNER 1: We're going to get her a large-screen TV! That way she can see it from her favorite recliner, and it will be large enough that she can finally enjoy TV. Her eyes are so bad, and this way she won't have to sit two feet in front of it.

PARTNER 2: Yeah, I wish we had one ourselves, but how are we going to afford that? We don't have enough time between now and Christmas to save that much money. It would have been a fantastic idea if you had thought about it in January, and we could have saved money for it.

PARTNER 1: Well, Wal-Mart has one on sale for $799. It's the best price I've seen yet. The problem is it's only on sale for this week. Don't you think it's a great idea?

PARTNER 2: *[astonished]* We don't have eight hundred dollars to spend! We only have about half that much in our savings, and *you said* we were going to keep that in case the oil bills get too high this winter.

PARTNER 1: *[whining]* I know, but we can just put it on our credit card. That way we can take advantage of this great sale.

PARTNER 2: *[hesitantly]* I don't know, dear; it's a great idea, but that's a lot of money for us to be paying off on a credit card. Even at our good rate, it's going to take us a year. Why don't we get something else this year and then save for it for next year?

PARTNER 1: *[pouting somewhat]* But I had such a good idea, and it's such a great sale. Just this once. Think of what a nice Christmas it will be with us not having to worry what to get my mom. She'll love it! And just think, my brother certainly can't match anything this nice.

PARTNER 2: Yeah, I guess you're right. OK, let's do it! Why wait when we can have it today?

III. CHRISTMAS CAROL CRISIS

[Three people are sitting at a table with hymn books, Bibles, and paper.]

PASTOR: Hey, guys, thanks for being willing to serve on the worship team with me during Advent. It's always such a hard season to plan, and I'm glad both of you could help me out.

TEAM MEMBER 1: Well, I don't know too much about Advent. Except every year we light the wreath at the altar. And I know we have a different family read something each Sunday. It's usually about light or hope or something like that, right?

TEAM MEMBER 2: Yeah! My family did it last year—I think on the third Sunday. It was something about hope. I remember the kids kept saying, "I hope I get this for Christmas," and "I hope I get that for Christmas." I don't think that's what our reading was about though. *[Everyone laughs.]*

PASTOR: Well, Advent is a time of preparation, and the focus is often on Mary and Joseph and God's promise of the Messiah. I've got some ideas here for each Sunday, so why don't we look at some hymns to go along with them?

TEAM MEMBER 1: Yeah, I love Christmas carols. One of my favorites is "It Came upon a Midnight Clear." When do you want to do that one? Maybe the first week?

TEAM MEMBER 2: I like that, too, but I think we should sing "Joy to the World" first to get us all ready for the season.

PASTOR: *[hesitantly]* Well, you know, I really don't want us to be singing Christmas carols during Advent. We'll sing those during Christmas.

TEAM MEMBER 1: *[incredulously]* What do you mean, we aren't going to sing Christmas carols now? We have all those Sundays in December when we can be singing them every week. It sure beats all the secular music we hear in the mall!

TEAM MEMBER 2: Yeah, anyway! We always sing those favorites like "Silent Night" and "The First Noel." If you don't put those in, why, folks are really going to be upset. They are good old standbys for the season.

PASTOR: I hear what you're saying, but maybe we need to lead the church in waiting for Christ this year—we can help them learn about the true meaning of Advent. After all, there is a lot to be gained in waiting.

TEAM MEMBERS 1 AND 2: *[astonished]* There is!?! *[Everyone freezes.]*

APPENDIX B

SONG ACCOMPANIMENTS

We Gather Here

For cantor, congregation, piano (or folk harp)
*rainstick & wind chimes (ad lib.)

Daryl Hollinger

meet our Sav-iour here.

Be Thou My Vision

Traditional Irish Melody
arr. Daryl Hollinger

Be thou my vi-sion, O Lord of my heart; naught be all else to me, save that thou art: thou my best thought, both by day and by night,

wak-ing or sleep-ing, thy pres-ence my light.

The God of Abraham Praise

Arr. Daryl Hollinger

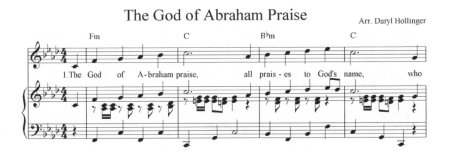

1.The God of A-braham praise, all prais-es to God's name, who

was and is and is to be, for - e'er the same! The

one e-ter-nal God, be-fore what now ap-pears; the

First, the Last: be-yond all thought through time - less years!

We Are Climbing Jacob's Ladder

African American Spiritual
arr. Daryl Hollinger

Out of the Shadows

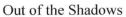

Daryl Hollinger

*Rit. and fermato last time only

NOTES

CHAPTER 1: THE SMALL CHURCH

1. While there is no clear definition of "emerging church," generally speaking, emerging or emergent Christianity relates to the dialogue between Christians and postmodernism, involving the focus on experience rather than doctrine, as well as the embrace of varieties of Christian worship and music. Emerging Christianity is committed to affirming pluralism, personal experience and testimony, and mission as essential to a living Christian faith in the twenty-first century.

2. In addition to hosting the Calvin Institute of Christian Worship program "Enlivening Worship and Music in the Small Church," Lancaster Theological Seminary sponsors programs in ministerial spirituality, excellence, and transformation for new pastors, pastors in midcareer, and pastors anticipating retirement, initially made possible by grants from the Lilly Endowment Program in Religion, under the direction of Craig Dykstra and John Wimmer. For more on Lancaster Theological Seminary's lay and clergy education and renewal program, consult *www.lancasterseminary.edu*.

3. Peter Bush and Christine O'Reilly, *Where Twenty or Thirty Are Gathered: Leading Worship in the Small Church* (Herndon, Va.: Alban Institute: 2006), vii.

4. Bush and O'Reilly, *Where Twenty or Thirty Are Gathered*, 5.

5. Bush and O'Reilly, *Where Twenty or Thirty Are Gathered*, x.

6. In this book, global music is defined as "songs outside the normative Euro-American heritage" (see Michael Hawn, *Halle, Halle: We Sing the World Round* [Garland, Texas: Choristers Guild, 1995], 5).

7. John Fawcett, "Blest Be the Tie that Binds" (1872).

8. Bush and O'Reilly, *Where Twenty or Thirty Are Gathered*, xiii.

9. Bush and O'Reilly, *Where Twenty or Thirty Are Gathered*, 5.

10. For more on the power of affirmations to transform people and con-gregations, see Bruce Epperly, *Holy Adventure: Forty-one Days of Audacious Living* (Nashville: Upper Room, 2008), and Bruce Epperly, *The Power of Affirmative Faith* (St. Louis: Chalice Press, 2001).

CHAPTER 2: GLORY AND GRATITUDE AND PRAISE

1. Alfred North Whitehead, *Science and the Modern World* (New York: Free Press, 1967), 192.

2. John Bell, *Come All You People*, from the Iona Community (Chicago: GIA Publications, Inc., 1994), 80.

3. Quoted in Roberta Bondi, *To Pray and to Love: Conversations on Prayer with the Early Church* (Minneapolis: Fortress, 1991), 25.

4. Gerald May, *The Awakened Heart: Opening Yourself to the Love You Need* (New York: HarperSanFrancisco, 1991).

5. Maltbie D. Babcock, "This Is My Father's World" (1901), *Chalice Hymnal* version (1995).

6. Catherine Cameron, "God Who Stretched the Spangled Heavens" (1967).

7. Martin Rinkart, "Now Thank We All Our God" (1636); tr. Cath-erine Winkworth (1858).

8. Al Carmines, "Many Gifts, One Spirit" (1973), also known as "God of Change and Glory"; words and music copyright © 1974 by Al Carmines; quotation used by permission of Edward Carmines.

9. Thomas Ken, "Praise God from Whom All Blessings Flow" (1674). Some congregations conclude the Doxology by singing the alternative "Cre-ator, Christ, and Holy Ghost."

CHAPTER 3: HOW CAN WE KEEP FROM SINGING?

1. Brian Wren, *Praying Twice: The Music and Words of Congregational Song* (Louisville: Westminster John Knox Press, 2000), 71.

2. Wren, *Praying Twice*, 17.

3. Michael Hawn, *Halle, Halle: We Sing the World Round* (Garland, Texas: Choristers Guild, 1999), 15–17.

4. A *djembe* is a goblet-shaped wooden drum, covered with goatskin and played with bare hands. It originated in West Africa.

5. Kristen L. Forman, *The New Century Hymnal Companion* (Cleve-land: Pilgrim Press, 1998), 421.

6. Kristine Forney and Joseph Machlis, *The Enjoyment of Music* (New York: W. W. Norton, 2007), A24.

7. Forney and Machlis, *The Enjoyment of Music*, 87.

8. John Bell, "Be Still and Know," from *There Is One Among Us* (copyright © 1999, Wild Goose Resource Group, Iona Community, Scotland; GIA Publications, Inc., exclusive North American agent), 17.

9. Bobby Fisher and Ziggy Stardust, "The Servant Song," *Gather Comprehensive 2nd Edition* (Chicago: GIA Publications, 1994), 489.

10. Priscilla J. Owens, "Jesus Saves" (1868); tune by William J. Kirkpatrick (1882).

11. *Worship and Service Hymnal* (Carol Stream, Ill.: Hope Publishing Co.), copyright © 1957.

12. Linda Clark, Joanne Swenson, and Mark Stamm, *How We Seek God Together* (Herndon, Va.: Alban Institute, 2001), 17.

13. Michael Hawn, *One Bread, One Body: Exploring Cultural Diversity in Worship* (Herndon, Va.: Alban Institute, 2003), 18.

14. Thomas Long, *Beyond the Worship Wars* (Herndon, Va.: Alban Institute, 2001), 13.

15. Hawn, *Halle, Halle*, 4.

16. Hawn, *One Bread, One Body*, part I.

17. Bruce Wilkenson, *Prayer of Jabez* (Portland, Ore.: Multnomah Press, 2000). Sold over nine million copies and became a *New York Times* best seller.

CHAPTER 4: THE WORK OF THE PEOPLE

1. Wren, *Praying Twice*, 50–54.

2. Text and music: Michael Joncas (1979); *Evangelical Lutheran Worship* (Minneapolis: Augsburg Fortress, 1998), #787.

3. Terri McClean, *New Harmonies* (Herndon, Va.: Alban Institute, 1998).

4. Alice Parker, *Melodious Accord: Good Singing in Church* (Chicago: Liturgical Training Publications, 1991), 83.

5. Parker, *Melodious Accord*, 6–7.

CHAPTER 5: SING TO GOD A NEW SONG

1. Jack Schrader, *Amazing Grace: Blues Gospel Piano* (Carol Stream, Ill.: Hope Publishing Co., 2001).

2. Hawn, *Halle, Halle* (CD).

3. Hawn, *Halle, Halle*, 7–8.

4. Hawn, *Halle, Halle* (teacher's edition), 4.

5. Robert Buckley Farlee, ed., *Leading the Church's Song* (Minneapolis: Augsburg Fortress, 1998), 109.

6. Hawn, *Halle, Halle* (CD).

7. John Bell and Alison Adam: *Sing with the World: Global Songs for Children* (Chicago: GIA Publications, 2003), 43 and CD.

8. Bell and Adam, *Sing with the World* (CD).

9. Tzu-chen Chao (b. 1888), "Golden Breaks the Dawn"; Chinese folk tune harm. by Bliss Wiant (1936); *New Century Hymnal* (Cleveland: Pilgrim Press, 1995), #470.

10. Scott Ressman, ed., *Sing! Prayer and Praise* (Cleveland: Pilgrim Press, 2009).

11. Robert Buckley Farlee, ed., *Leading the Church's Song* (Minneapolis: Augsburg Fortress, 1998), 83.

12. McClean, *New Harmonies*.

13. McClean, *New Harmonies*.

14. Graham Kendrick, "Amazing Love" (1986), *Worship and Praise Songbook* (Minneapolis: Augsburg Fortress, 1999), 8.

CHAPTER 6: THE PASTOR AND THE CHURCH MUSICIAN

1. "Pastor Fred" is a pseudonym; the anecdote describing an encounter Daryl once had with a senior pastor draws as well on many encounters that church musicians and pastors have shared with us.

2. For more on Myers-Briggs Personality Type Indicator and its role in healthy ministerial relationships, see Bruce and Katherine Epperly, *Feed the Fire: Avoiding Clergy Burnout* (Cleveland: Pilgrim, 2008), 139–158; Otto Kroeger and Roy Oswald, *Personality Type and Religious Leadership* (Herndon, Va.: Alban Institute, 1988); and Otto Kroeger and Janet Thuesen, *Type Talk: The 16 Personality Types that Determine How We Live, Love, and Work* (New York: Dell, 1988).

3. For more on the spiritual aspects of the regular tasks of pastoral ministry—teaching, preaching, worship leadership, spiritual formation, pastoral care, administration, and prophetic hospitality—see Bruce and Katherine Epperly, *Tending to the Holy: The Practice of the Presence of God in Ministry* (Herndon, Va.: Alban Institute, 2009).

4. For more on pastoral spirituality, see Epperly and Epperly, *Feed the Fire*; Epperly and Epperly, *Four Seasons of Ministry: Gathering a Harvest of Righteousness* (Herndon, Va.: Alban Institute, 2008); and Epperly and Epperly, *Tending to the Holy*.

CHAPTER 7: WORSHIP PLANNING

1. Jacques Berthier, *Songs and Prayers from Taize* (Chicago: GIA Publications, 1991), 12.

2. Robert Webber, *Planning Blended Worship: The Creative Mixture of Old and New* (Nashville: Abington, 1998).

3. *Evangelical Lutheran Worship* (Minneapolis: Augsburg Fortress, 1998), 97.

4. Kristine Forney and Joseph Machlis, *The Enjoyment of Music*, 27.

CHAPTER 8: THEOLOGY FOR THE CHURCH MUSICIAN

1. Church of the Province of New Zealand, *A New Zealand Prayer Book* (Auckland and London: Collins, 1989), 481; also cited in *The New Century Hymnal* (Cleveland: Pilgrim Press, 1995), #886.

2. *The New Century Hymnal*, #882.

3. *The New Century Hymnal*, #885.

4. For more on appreciative inquiry, see David L. Cooperrider and Diana Whitney, *Appreciative Inquiry: A Positive Revolution in Change* (San Francisco: Barrett-Koehler Publishers, 2005); Mark Lau Branson, *Memories, Hopes, and Conversations* (Herndon, Va.: Alban Institute, 2004); and Robert J. Voyle and Kim M. Voyle, *The Appreciative Way: An Introduction to Appreciative Inquiry for Work and Daily Living* (Hillsboro, Ore.: Clergy Leadership Institute, 2006).

CHAPTER 9: GREAT IS GOD'S FAITHFULNESS

1. Craig Dykstra, "Pastoral and Ecclesial Imagination" in Craig Dykstra and Dorothy Bass, *Life Abundant: Practical Theology, Theological Education, and Christian Ministry* (Grand Rapids: Eerdmans, 2008), 57.

2. Henri F. Hemy, "Faith of Our Fathers," (1864), adapt. James G. Walton, 1874; public domain; see updated version "Faith of the Martyrs" in *The New Century Hymnal*, #381.

3. Horatio G. Spofford, "It Is Well with My Soul" (1873); music by Philip P. Bliss (1876).

4. Thomas O. Chisholm, "Great Is Thy Faithfulness" (1923); music by William M. Runyon (1923); copyright 1923; © renewed 1951 by Hope Publishing Co.

5. Civilla D. Martin, "His Eye Is on the Sparrow" (1905); music by Charles H. Gabriel (1905).

6. Alfred North Whitehead, *Process and Reality: Corrected Edition* (New York: Free Press, 1979), 338–339.

7. Henry F. Lyte, "Abide with Me" (1847); music by William Henry Monk (1861).

8. Alfred North Whitehead, *Process and Reality*, 351.

9. John C. Ylvisaker, "I Was There to Hear Your Borning Cry." Text and music copyright © 1985 by John C. Ylvisaker, Box 321, Waverly IA 50677, (319) 352-4396. Used by permission.

10. Fred Kaan, "Let Us Talents and Tongues Employ" (1975); music, Jamaican folk melody, adapt. Doreen Potter (1975).

11. *United Church of Christ Worship Book* (New York: United Church of Christ Office of Church Life and Leadership, 1986), 367.

12. Victor Frankl, *Man's Search For Meaning* (Boston: Beacon Press, 1959), 65.

13. *United Church of Christ Worship Book*, 372.

14. Dag Hammarskjold, *Markings* (New York: Vintage, 2006), 89.

15. Thomas O. Chisholm, "Living for Jesus" (1917); music, C. Harold Lowden (1915); public domain.

CHAPTER 10: A TALE OF TWO CHURCHES

1. Henri Nouwen, *Jesus: A Gospel* (Maryknoll, N.Y.: Orbis Books, 2001), 7.

2. This section has been adapted from Bruce and Kate Epperly, "Emerging Process: Worship as Ancient-Future-Now," *Creative Transformation* 16:4 (Fall 2007): 8–11.

3. For more on Disciples United Community Church, consult the website www.ducc.us.

4. According to Wikipedia.org, "LGBT (or GLBT) is an initialism referring collectively to lesbian, gay, bisexual, and transgender people. . . . A popular variant adds the letter Q for queer and questioning. . . . The acronym has become mainstream as a self-designation and has been adopted by the majority of LGBT community centers and LGBT media in many English-speaking countries."

5. For more on the healings of Jesus and healing worship, see Bruce Epperly, *God's Touch: Faith, Wholeness, and the Healing Miracles of Jesus* (Louisville: Westminster/John Knox, 2001), and Epperly, *Healing Worship: Purpose and Practice* (Cleveland: Pilgrim Press, 2006).

6. For more on reiki, see Bruce and Katherine Epperly, *Reiki Healing Touch and the Way of Jesus* (Kelowna, British Columbia: Northstone, 2005). Reiki is a type of hands-on healing touch, grounded in Japanese and Chinese traditional medicine.